POETIC DICTION

Other books by Owen Barfield

PUBLISHED BY WESLEYAN UNIVERSITY PRESS:

History, Guilt, and Habit

The Rediscovery of Meaning and Other Essays

What Coleridge Thought

Speaker's Meaning

Romanticism Comes of Age

Unancestral Voice

Worlds Apart

Saving the Appearances

Owen Barfield on C. S. Lewis

A Barfield Reader

PUBLISHED ELSEWHERE:

History in English Words

Eager Spring

Orpheus: A Poetic Drama

Owen Barfield and the Origin of Language

POETIC DICTION

a study in meaning

by

OWEN BARFIELD

Foreword by Howard Nemerov
Afterword by the author

Wesleyan University Press

PUBLISHED BY UNIVERSITY PRESS OF NEW ENGLAND

HANOVER AND LONDON

Poetic Diction was first published by Faber and Gwyer, Ltd., in 1928; a second edition was published by Faber and Faber, Ltd., in 1952.

LIBRARY OF CONGRESS CATALOGING-IN-PUBLICATION DATA
Barfield, Owen, 1898–
Poetic diction.

Includes bibliographical references and index.
1. Poetry. 2. Style, Literary I. Title.
[PN1031.B3 1987] 808.1 87–22985
ISBN 0–8195–6026–x (pbk.)

WESLEYAN PAPERBACK
Printed in the United States of America
First Wesleyan edition, 1973
second edition, 1984

10 9 8 7 6

To

C. S. LEWIS

'*Opposition is true friendship*'

CONTENTS

	FOREWORD BY HOWARD NEMEROV	*page* 1
	PREFACE TO FIRST EDITION	11
	PREFACE TO SECOND EDITION	14
I	DEFINITION AND EXAMPLES	41
II	THE EFFECTS OF POETRY	47
III	METAPHOR	60
IV	MEANING AND MYTH	77
V	LANGUAGE AND POETRY	93
VI	THE POET	102
VII	THE MAKING OF MEANING (I)	111
VIII	THE MAKING OF MEANING (II)	127
IX	VERSE AND PROSE	145
X	ARCHAISM	152
XI	STRANGENESS	168
XII	CONCLUSION	178
	APPENDIX I	182
	APPENDIX II	183
	APPENDIX III	197
	APPENDIX IV	203
	AFTERWORD	212
	INDEX	226

FOREWORD

This book first appeared in England in 1928, and was reissued there in 1952 with the addition of a new preface (here included) that helped to specify the application of its author's argument to views of the subject that had in the interval become more explicit, more brutal, and more unthinkingly accepted by scholar and layman alike, than had previously appeared possible.

Among the few poets and teachers of my acquaintance who know POETIC DICTION it has been valued not only as a secret book, but nearly as a sacred one; with a certain sense that its teaching was quite properly esoteric, not as the possession of a few snobs but as something that would easily fail of being understood by even the most learned of those jugheads whose mouths continually pour forth but whose ears will serve only for carrying purposes.

It is not for the prefator to anticipate the arguments of the book, which the reader perhaps should already be learning at first hand by abandoning me in favor of Mr. Barfield; maybe the only preface worth having would be one such as I saw in a manual of Buddhism: that said, in effect, if you have read this far, throw the book away, it's not for you. But it may be appropriate to introduce the American edition of Owen Barfield's book with some reflections on its subject, and on the situation of that subject at the present time.

Foreword

It seems as though there are two main ways of taking poetic diction as a subject of study. In the first of these, it is a technical matter belonging to the art of poetry, or, more exactly, to the craft of poetry, hence of interest only to poets, perhaps especially to young poets who learn according to their natures a certain boldness, or a certain fastidiousness, pertaining to what is possible and what is forbidden in the art when they first begin to practice it. At present, for example, the poet in his character of angler will not allow himself to speak about fish as "the finny prey." He would feel silly if he did, and quite properly so; he would *be* silly if he did.

But even at this early stage a little reflection may cause him to ask himself why, if "the finny prey" is now impossible, prohibited, *out*, could it ever have been *in*? How could it ever have appeared to any poet seemly, appropriate, and—in a word that raises at once more questions than can be answered—*natural*?

If the poet is of a reflective and inquiring disposition—there is no guarantee that this is poetically a good thing for him to be—he senses very soon that a question of this kind, if he will pursue it, is going to take him into some very queer and even perilous places. "For," he may say to himself, "here is my language, that all this time I have just been using as if—as if—as if what? Why, as if it were natural, as if the words really belonged to the things, as if the words were really the 'souls' of things, their essences or Logoi, and not by any means the mere conventional tags they are so often said to be."

At this point the first way of regarding poetic diction, as a study in technique, goes over into the second, where the subject becomes psychological, metaphysical, and extremely problematic. Here the poet, especially if he is still young, may find it best to abandon the inquiry in favor of writing poems while he yet is able to, agreeing with something Mr. Barfield says in another connection: "The fact that the meanings of words change, not only from age to age, but from context to context, is certainly interesting; but it is interesting solely because it is a nuisance."

But when the poet is older, if he has continued to write, it is at least probable that he will reach a point, either a stopping point or a turning point, at which he finds it necessary to inquire into the sense of what he has been doing, and now the question of poetic diction becomes for him supremely important, nothing less than the question of primary perception, of imagination itself, of how thought ever emerged (if it did) out of a world of things. There is some evidence that poets reaching this point—I think for example of Yeats, Valéry, Stevens—may feel acutely their want of formal philosophical training, so that they either abandon poetry and turn to study for a time, or else direct their poetry itself toward this study. And yet it seems their want of formal training may be not altogether a disadvantage, so that any regret they may express on the subject will perhaps have something of the irony of Socrates, who introduces his own reflections on names and natures by saying, "If I had not been poor, I might have heard the fifty-drachma course of the great Prodicus, which is a complete education in grammar and language—these are his own words—and then I should have been at once able to answer your question about the correctness of names. But, indeed, I have only heard the one-drachma course, and therefore I do not know the truth about such matters." (Cratylus, 384b).

Now this development of the subject of poetic diction in the individual poet, as it were from five-finger exercises to questions of life and death, shows an odd and suggestive correspondence with a part of the course of poetry in English. It might be said that in the youth of our poetry the imagination was mysterious but not problematic, while later on, roughly from the time of the French Revolution, the problematic nature of imagination, the making explicit of its mystery, began to be the chief preoccupation of poets and even the subject of their poetic meditation; for example, The Prelude, a poem about writing poetry, Blake's *Milton* or his *Jerusalem*, Keats' Grecian Urn Ode.

In Shakespeare's time, as Rosemond Tuve has taught us (*Elizabethan and Metaphysical Imagery*), poetic diction was scarcely distinguished as a subject by itself, but belonged to the study of rhetoric, the making of tropes and distinguishing of figures, and was learned by the poets, as by other men, of school masters, and in the grammar school. Consciously, by analysis of the devices of speech, the student learned the recipes appropriate to the producing of particular effects, of grandeur, violence, sweetness, or whatever. The sturdy common sense of the attitude is delightfully represented by Ben Jonson: *Ingenium*, "a natural wit and a Poeticall nature in chiefe," is indeed his first requirement of a poet, but the others all have to do with conscious technical mastery. *Exercitatio* is one: "If then it succeed not, cast not away the Quills yet, nor scratch the Wainescott, beate not the poor Deske, but bring all to the forge, and file again; tourne it anew. There is no statute Law of the Kingdome bids you bee a poet against your will; or the first quarter. If it come, in a yeare or two, it is well." *Imitatio* is another: "to bee able to convert the substance or Riches of another Poet to his owne use." And last is *Lectio*, "exactneese of Studie and multiplicity of reading. . . . not alone enabling him to know the History or Argument of a Poeme and to report it, but so to master the matter and Stile, as to shew hee knows how to handle, place, or dispose of either with Elegancie when need shall bee."

The immense distance of this attitude from most modern attitudes to the study of poetry is as impressive as it is obvious; when Jonson adds that a man must not think to become a poet "by dreaming hee hath been in Parnassus, or having washt his lips, as they say, in Helicon," the modern student may think with a profitable amazement of this warning in relation to, say, Shelley, Baudelaire, Verhaeren, Rilke, and so on.

In the seventeenth and eighteenth centuries it would appear that prose and poetry, which had formerly been rather close together in their choice of language, were decisively differentiated from one another, and there gradually grew up a kind of language special to poetry and not admissible in prose except on most exalted occasions. This language gives, historically, the first separable meaning to the term "poetic diction." And for a long while it is assumed that this state of affairs is natural, necessary, and reasonable; nor do poets much inquire why it should be thus and not otherwise. When Pope writes, "We acknowledge Homer the father of poetical diction, the first who taught *that language of the Gods* to men" (his italics), the second clause does not appear to him, though it does to us, as requiring elaboration. Just as early modern historians had perforce to pretend that the peoples they studied had suddenly appeared out of nowhere and begun to be "historical," so Pope sensibly assumes there is no point in staring at the darkness inside that phrase about the language of the Gods, and decides instead to look at Homer's diction, which is something he can see.

But it may be that the truly "modern" thing about the modern age, the nineteenth century and the twentieth, its really diagnostic trait, is the interest in beginnings, in origin, in aetiology: when we try to say what something *is*—witness Darwin, for example, and Freud—our way of doing it is to go back and talk about how it got to be the way it looks now. Or it might be said that with the eroding away of the assumptions of the first chapters of Genesis, other mythology had to be supplied, mythology in the fashionable scientific language, if only in order to fill up what began to appear as the dark backward and abysm of time.

The great change in the consciousness, or self-consciousness, of the Western world that is usually dated to the French Revolution appears simultaneously in letters as the Romantic movement, or revolt; and this revolt has first and last a great deal to do with poetic diction in the first, or technical, sense; it is a revolt against a conventional language that has precipitated out conventions of feeling and belief. To Wordsworth, writing in 1800, the term itself is a sort of insult: "There will also be found in these pieces little of what is usually called poetic diction; I have taken as much pains to avoid it as others ordinarily take to produce it."

But it belongs to the understanding of Romanticism that you cannot rebel merely against the technical, or craft, part of poetry without rebelling also against something deeper and of more generally human concern, the belief about the world and the place of mankind in the world that produced the technical conventions you find intolerable; and this rebellion, if thoroughly pursued, involves the rebel in making his own creation myth, his own story of how things came to be as they are.

In an appendix to his "Observations Prefixed to the Second Edition of Lyrical Ballads," Wordsworth elaborates on the subject of poetic diction, and his way of doing it takes him back to first things: "The earliest poets of all nations generally wrote from passion excited by real events; they wrote naturally, and as men: feeling powerfully as they did, their language was daring, and figurative." William Blake, a few years earlier, testifies in a similar way: "The ancient Poets animated all sensible objects with Gods or geniuses, calling them by the names and adorning them with the properties of woods, rivers, mountains, lakes, cities, nations, and whatever their enlarged and numerous senses could perceive." One of his examples is Isaiah, who is made to say, about the divine vision, "I saw no God, nor heard any, in a finite organical perception; but my senses discover'd the infinite in everything. . . ."

About these earliest and ancient poets, Mr. Barfield has much to say, which I must not anticipate; it is enough to make my present point if I add that the subsequent intellectualizing imitation of the supposed practice of the supposed earliest poets produces, for Wordsworth, the corruption of language that he means by "poetic diction," and, for Blake, systematic abstraction, priesthood, scientism, the loss of the good of the imagination.

For the great Romantics, then, poetic diction becomes a

subject of the first importance, because out of their efforts to reform this highly specialized diction and reach back instead to "nature" arose the deeper question of the extent of the imagination's role as creator of the visible and sensible world. For Blake that extent was total: Imagination is the Savior. For Wordsworth the relation was a more tentative and balancing one, in which world and thought were mutually adjusted one to another, a solution about which Blake wrote: "You shall not bring me down to believe such fitting & fitted. I know better & please your Lordship." For both, and for their great contemporaries, the primacy of imagination was a point of considerable anxiety, too, because the view opposed, the view of a universe of independently and fatally moving *things*, the view named by Alfred North Whitehead as "scientific materialism," was so evidently triumphant in imposing its claims upon the general mind of Europe and America.

That view has continued triumphant, though disturbing questions are ever more persistently raised about its foundations. And in the situation of poetry at present, in the United States, it appears as though one after another outbreak of "modernism" which regards itself specifically as anti-romantic presently reveals that it is but another variation on superficial aspects of the Romantic movement, while something submerged and unfinished about that movement remains largely untouched. Poetry and criticism, with a few honorable exceptions, either disregard the question raised about the imagination, or else seem to assume implicitly, without saying much, some positivist or behaviorist or mechanist resolution of it, and one result in particular is apparent: a poetry enthralled by the false realism of the reason, spellbound to the merely picturesque, imposed upon, Blake would have said, by the phantasy of the angel whose works are only Analytics, and so prevented, in spite of all its claims and manifestoes, from dreaming deeply or other than the common dream.

It is to the student willing to open this question of the imagination again to a candid exploration that Owen Barfield's book is directed.

HOWARD NEMEROV

PREFACE TO THE FIRST EDITION

Readers of this book may possibly be assisted by a few brief remarks on its form. This is, or was intended to be, broadly speaking, a progress from phenomena to general principles, and from those general principles back again to phenomena. The initial phenomena are the author's own aesthetic and psychological experiences: while those, to which the general principles induced from these are subsequently applied, are various problems of literature and especially of 'poetic diction' in its narrower sense. The 'general principles', however, for reasons explained in the book itself, take the form rather of pictures and metaphors than of propositions. Moreover, owing to their discrepancy from many opinions which are very commonly regarded—not on aesthetic grounds—as definitely established, much more time has been spent in developing and defending them than would ordinarily have been necessary in a short work on Poetic Diction.

I may perhaps be allowed to add that this progress is not simply adopted artificially, for the purpose of appearing scientific, but is, roughly, an autobiographical record of the manner in which the author arrived at the general principles in question; for when he first began to enjoy poetry, he really had no beliefs about it or general principles of interpretation at all. An early perception that poetry reacts on the meanings of the words it employs was followed by a dim, yet apodeictically certain, conviction that there are 'two sorts of poetry'; and a series of unsuccessful attempts to rationalize these and other aesthetic experiences in terms of the various theories of language, literature, and life, with which the author happened to come in touch, resulted in the present volume.

Having concluded it, I am confronted with a problem which many Europeans, I fancy, are likely to have to face, as time passes—that of defining the precise nature of the debt owed by the book to the late Dr. Rudolf Steiner. Begun as an academic exercise a good many years ago, it was subsequently dropped, and it was in the interval that I came across Steiner's work. And now I am in difficulties. For, while the references and quotations in the Appendices must convey an absurdly inadequate sense of what this meant, yet it would, it seems, be impossible in a Preface to convey half *my own* sense of indebtedness without appearing, quite improperly, to father upon him many of the views on poetry which I have expressed—whereas I can scarcely recollect anything he has said or written on that subject at all, nor am I yet acquainted with his lectures on Language. I may possibly be excused, therefore, for abandoning the problem altogether. In any case, only those who are themselves more than superficially acquainted with Steiner's work would be able to gauge the inestimable advantage of being even partly in touch with it, to anyone engaged on either the theory or the practice of any art.

The appearance of Spengler's *Decline of the West*, a profound and alarmingly learned study of the *historical*—as opposed to the *literary*—relation between prosaic and poetic, which occurred just after this book was completed in its original academic form, interested me so much that, in revising it for the press, I have added two or three allusions.

Finally, I would ask those who may object to the theory of poetry developed here, that it takes no account of *feeling*, to recollect that the kind of inspired thinking which I have attempted to depict, *assumes* the utmost intensity of feeling as a necessary pre-requisite. There could be no other way of reaching it. It can only begin when feeling has become too powerful to remain only personal, so that the individual is compelled by his human nature, either to THINK in reality, or to find, more or less instinctively, some suitable device for dimming his consciousness.

OWEN BARFIELD

1927

PREFACE TO THE SECOND EDITION

The Preface to the first edition described briefly how this book grew out of two empirical observations, first, that poetry reacts on the meanings of the words it employs, and, secondly, that there appear to be two sorts of poetry. The book itself, with it's sub-title 'A Study in Meaning', was an attempt to rationalize these observations in terms of 'the various theories of language, life and literature with which the author happened to come in touch'. Thus, it claims to present, not merely a theory of poetic diction, but a theory of poetry: and not merely a theory of poetry, but a theory of knowledge. It is as such, I see, that it must be judged. Apparently the author was determined that the title at least should be unassuming.

Twenty-three years having elapsed since the first appearance of *Poetic Diction*, this second edition is offered, with a few trifling revisions, to a generation which is much less interested in those 'various theories' than its immediate predecessor; which has indeed been encouraged to regard them as irrelevant to its own more maturely sceptical philosophy. Father, it says, rather patronizingly, was all right in his way; it is not so much that he was wrong, but he 'asked the wrong questions'. This is confidently affirmed no less of Kant than of Berkeley, and no less of Locke than of Kant.

If I were writing *Poetic Diction* today, therefore, it would be the ideas of Hume and his more recent disciples, rather than those of Locke and Kant, that I should feel impelled to criticize in the Appendices; and not the less so because, at the moment of writing, the fashionable method is to analyse language itself—which is the heart of my matter. I propose accordingly to attempt such a criticism here; and I would tentatively advise any reader who may be coming quite fresh to the subject to turn at this point to Chapter One, resuming this Preface, if he still has a mind to it, after following the argument which is developed in the book itself.

I must first mention a theory of the nature of language, popularized by Dr. I. A. Richards since this book appeared, though a good deal less is heard of it today. This is the division of meaning into the two classes, 'emotive' and 'referential.' The language of science, it is said, may be veridical, because the words it uses have a 'referent', that is, they refer to something real. But the figurative language of poetry has no referent, its sole function is to arouse emotion and it is therefore without veridical significance.

If the following pages show anything at all, they show that this doctrine, if it could be believed, would write off as emotive and without veridical significance practically all the abstract words in our language (for at what particular point in their history did they acquire a referent?) including, naturally, such words as *meaning, verify, emotive and referential*. Others, besides myself, have pointed this out, and the fallacious distinction was exhaustively criticized in

Mr. D. G. James's book, *Scepticism and Poetry*.[1] But I do not think it is for that reason that we are now hearing less of the theory. It is a failing common to a good many contemporary metaphysical theories that they can be applied to all things except themselves but that, when so applied, they extinguish themselves; and experience has taught me that, when men are really attached to such a theory, most of them will, after this has been pointed out to them, continue nevertheless to apply it to all things (except it itself). The reason is rather that those who must think about language and the world in that particular way have gone further since then and abolished the idea of a 'referent' altogether.

Now in a footnote to page 113 of this book it is pointed out that 'logical judgements, by their nature, can only *render more explicit* some one part of a truth *already implicit in their terms*'. And in another, to page 131, that the logician is continually seeking to reduce the meaning of his terms, and that 'he could only evolve a language whose propositions would really obey the laws of thought by eliminating meaning altogether'. I do not think it too sweeping to say that the doctrines of linguistic analysis, or as it has sometimes been called, Logical Positivism, are no more than an extensive gloss on this principle.

Its corollary, that all the propositions of logic are mere tautologies, is the heart of Wittgenstein's *Tractatus Logico-Philosophicus*[2] which Bertrand Russell translated into English in 1922; and it is this broom with which it

[1] George Allen & Unwin, 1937.

[2] e.g. All propositions of logic say the same thing. That is, nothing. Proof in logic is only a mechanical expedient to facilitate the recognition of tautology, where it is complicated. Op. cit. 5, 43 and 6, 1262.

is hoped to sweep away, as meaningless, all statements not related to physically observable or verifiable events, to limit the sphere of man's knowledge to the increasingly tentative findings of physical science, and to dismiss all other affirmations as meaningless. For all propositions except those from which some observation-statement can be deduced are, it is averred, meaningless, either as misuse of language, or as tautologies.

Hume's philosophy differs from Locke's in the much smaller role which it assigns to the activity of the human mind. Locke begins, certainly, by denying the doctrine of 'innate ideas' and affirming the principle *nihil in intellectu quod non prius fuerit in sensu.* But although he says that there can be no idea without a previous perception, he does not quite take the further step of identifying the two. He writes of ideas as though they were something which appeared in the mind as a kind of response to sense-perceptions and—what is perhaps more important—his interest is concentrated on the activity of the mind in dealing with these ideas. The Wit, which combines, and the Judgement, which distinguishes them, are for him realities.

For Hume on the other hand the ideas *are* the percepts or, as he calls them, *impressions.* When a sense-impression loses its first vivacity, it becomes an idea, and there is no content of thought which was not originally a sense datum. The activity of the mind in memory or imagination is limited to 'retaining' the original impression; the memory with more, and the imagination with less 'force and vivacity.' For Hume therefore man, as knower, is above all a passive recipient of impressions. Such is also the assumption on which the edifice of physical science is erected.

In the days of Locke and Hume it was felt that science, the newcomer, required a foundation in philosophy; but since then the two have changed places. The startling and largely beneficent achievements of science in the practical business of manipulating matter and carting it to and fro have so impressed the mind of the empiricist that he is content to treat its ever-changing assumptions as 'given.' If he is a philosopher, he regards it as his business, not to question the scientific assumptions of the day, but rather to justify the ways of science to man.

There is however one assumption of physical science which has remained unchanged longer than the rest. It is still assumed by science (as it is by the man in the street) that the real world is a 'somewhat', in the construction of which the mind of man does not participate; of which it is purely a detached observer. To this view the philosophy of Hume is very relevant and, although that philosophy has actually been called the *reductio ad absurdum* of scepticism, his twentieth-century followers, compelled to vary the findings of philosophy to suit the assumptions of science, have sought to build on it.

It is of course in attempting to describe more precisely the nature of the 'somewhat' that science both parts company with the man in the street and keeps changing its ground. In the nineteenth century the real world was assumed to consist, in the last resort, of things. The things got smaller and smaller—molecules, atoms, electrons—but they were at least *there* and if you had a powerful enough microscope you would, it was assumed, see something like a number of billiard-balls, or little solar systems. So, in his less sophisticated way, Hume had been content to assume that the 'impressions' which were the material of knowledge were produced in the senses by 'objects'. Twentieth-century science has abolished the 'thing' altogether; and twentieth-century philosophy (that part of it, at least, which takes no account of imagination) has obediently followed suit. There are no objects, says the voice of Science, there are only bundles of waves—or possibly something else; adding that, although it is convenient to think of them, it would be naïve to suppose that the waves or the something else actually exist. There is no 'referent', echoes the philosophy of linguistic analysis deferentially, no substance or underlying reality which is 'meant' by words. There are only descriptions, only the words themselves, though it 'happens to be the case' that men have from the beginning so persistently supposed the contrary that they positively cannot open their mouths without doing so.

'It happens to be the case'—complains Mr. A. J. Ayer in his *Language, Truth and Logic*[1]—'that we cannot, in our language, refer to the sensible properties of a thing, without introducing a word or phrase which appears to stand for the thing itself as opposed to anything which may be said about it.'

Kant erected the Forms of Perception as a kind of impenetrable screen between the real world of 'things in themselves' and the mind of man. The Positivists have substituted syntax for the forms of perception, and scrapped the things as otiose.

It was not to be supposed that they would stop short here, or fail to see that the cardinal error of 'introducing

[1] Gollancz, 1950.

a word or phrase which appears to stand for the thing itself' applies with at least as much force to noumenal as to phenomenal 'things'. Such for example as the mind. When *Poetic Diction* was written, the existence of the mind as agent had recently been denied by the Behaviourists on psychological grounds. In his *The Concept of Mind*[1] Professor Gilbert Ryle reaches the same conclusion on grounds which he considers to be semantic, and I think it is worth pausing to summarize his argument. Very briefly it is this. A word such as *golf* (the example is my own) certainly has a meaning, and is a convenient general term to cover a whole ramshackle series of events. But the fact that words have meanings does not warrant our asking 'When and where do these meanings occur?' and it would be illusory to assume, because *golf* has a meaning, that there is a ghostly thing called 'golf' existing in a ghostly world of its own. Exactly the same argument applies to the word *mind*. The persistent notion which men have entertained of the mind as a somewhat in itself, as an autonomous agent, distinguishable from the body—or, as Professor Ryle himself puts it, as 'the ghost in the machine'—is an illusion based on a confusion arising from men's misunderstanding of the 'rules' of the very language which they themselves have made.

Nor can the mind be a sort of warehouse in which to store abstract ideas—for 'no one is ever heard to say he has just found an abstract idea after having mislaid it for some weeks'.

The author criticizes the use of such words as *experience* and *consciousness* as smacking of this illusion and denies

[1] Hutchinson, 1950.

altogether, and with irony, 'the hallowed antithesis beween the public, physical world and the private mental world'. It is not of course merely the metaphorical use of the word *world* which he quarrels with. His concern is to deny that there is such a thing as private experience at all. Nor has the obvious objection escaped him: 'how then does it come about that you do not feel the pain in my foot?' His manner of disposing of this objection, besides being a little breath-taking, affords a clear illustration of the analytical argument from tautology and syntax to which I have already referred. 'It is true,' says Professor Ryle, '*and even tautologous* that the cobbler cannot feel the shoe pinching me, unless the cobbler is myself, but this is not because he is excluded from a peep-show open only to me, but *because it would make no sense* to say that he was in my pain, and no sense, therefore, to say that he was noticing the tweak that I was having.' (My italics.)

I shall return to this, but must remark in passing that this attempt to dismiss the palpable by writing off as tautologous the language in which it is affirmed is surely one of the strangest that has ever bemused a vigorous mind. By the same device black (though it is perhaps better to avoid saying so, because it 'makes no sense') may be thought of as white; for to object that black is 'not white' is to found on a tautology. The theory is, that what is self-evident may for that very reason be profitably ignored.

Experience suggests to me that after the lapse of another twenty-three years the particular doctrines of linguistic analysis are unlikely to be a very live issue. If I seem to have given them disproportionate attention, it is because they are, to my mind, the typical contemporary outcrop of a subterranean vein of human response which is itself unlikely to peter out. On the contrary the conflicting theories of knowledge of which the following pages take cognizance show every sign of diverging more and more widely, leaving a deeper and deeper gulf of incomprehension between them. Between those for whom 'knowledge' means ignorant but effective power, and those for whom the individual imagination is the medium of all knowledge from perception upward, a truce will not readily be struck. Nor can we safely assume that the conflict will be confined to the intellectual arena. In the nineteenth century, belief in imagination proved itself to be clearly allied with belief in individual freedom; necessarily so, because the act of imagination is the individual mind exercising its sovereign unity. In the twentieth century we are gradually learning that the converse is equally true. There is a curiously aggressive note, often degenerating into a sneer, in the style of those who expound the principles of linguistic analysis. Before he even begins to write, the Logical Positivist has taken the step from 'I prefer not to interest myself in propositions which cannot be empirically verified' to 'all propositions which cannot be empirically verified are meaningless'. The next step to 'I shall legislate to prevent anyone else wasting his time on meaningless propositions' is unlikely to appear either illogical or negative to his successor in title. Those who mistake efficiency for meaning inevitably end by loving compulsion, even if it takes them, like Bernard Shaw, the best part of a lifetime to get there.

The author of *Man and Superman*, *Pygmalion*, *St. Joan*

has my unstinted homage, but that should not deter me from pointing out, in this context, that in the closing years which witnessed his leaning towards political dictatorship he developed an enthusiasm for the 'reform' of spelling, which he expressed with a vehemence bordering on mania and ultimately endowed with the bulk of his considerable estate. Of all devices for dragooning the human spirit, the least clumsy is to procure its abortion in the womb of language; and we should recognize, I think, that those—and their number is increasing—who are driven by an impulse to reduce the specifically human to a mechanical or animal regularity, will continue to be increasingly irritated by the nature of the mother tongue and make it their point of attack. The strategy is well advised. Language is the storehouse of imagination; it cannot continue to be itself without performing its function. But its function is, to mediate transition from the unindividualized, dreaming spirit that carried the infancy of the world to the individualized human spirit, which has the future in its charge. If therefore they succeed in expunging from language all the substance of its past, in which it is naturally so rich, and finally converting it into the species of algebra that is best adapted to the uses of indoctrination and empirical science, a long and important step forward will have been taken in the selfless cause of the liquidation of the human spirit.

I believe the difference between the two theories of knowledge may best be presented in a parable. Once upon a time there was a very large motor-car called the Universe. Although there was nobody who wasn't on board, nobody knew how it worked or how to work it, and in course of time two very different problems occupied the attention of two different groups of passengers. The first group became interested in invisibles like internal combustion; but the second group said the thing to do was to push and pull levers and find out by trial and error what happened. The words 'internal combustion', they said, were obviously meaningless, because nobody ever pushed or pulled either of these things. For a time both groups agreed that knowledge of how it worked and knowledge of how to work it were closely connected with one another, but in the end the second group began to maintain that the first kind of knowledge was an illusion based on a misunderstanding of language. Pushing, pulling and seeing what happens, they said, are not a means to knowledge; they *are* knowledge. It was an odd sort of car, because, after the second group had with conspicuous and gratifying success tried pushing and pulling all the big levers, they began on some of the smaller ones, and the car was so constructed that nearly all of these, whatever other effect they had, acted as accelerators. Meanwhile the first group held their breath and began to think that their kind of knowledge might perhaps come in useful after the smash.

The notion that knowledge consists of seeing what happens and getting used to it—as distinct from consciously participating in what *is*—was first worked out systematically by Hume. A mere sense-impression is something that happens to us, not something that we do, and Hume started from the assumption that thoughts themselves are faded sense-impressions. These simple ideas, he held, associate themselves more or less automatically in the mind by virtue of 'some associating quality', by which one idea naturally introduces another. There were three such qualities, namely *resemblance*, *contiguity*, and *causation*.

The fatal flaw in these premisses has often been pointed out, namely, that the idea or experience of *resemblance* (and the same is true of the other two and indeed of all relations) cannot itself have originated as a sense-impression. This is a fact of which every mind capable of grasping the nature of thought can become aware by reflection. With those who, after the appearance of reflection, maintain the contrary no argument is possible. 'Whoever', wrote Locke, 'reflects on what passes in his own mind cannot miss it; and if he does not reflect, all the words in the world cannot make him have any notion of it.' As to Hume himself, he seems never to have directed his attention to the point. I shall only add that the perception of resemblance, the demand for unity, is at all levels the proper activity of the imagination, or—as I have called it elsewhere in this book—concrete thinking.

This is the crux of the two conflicting theories of knowledge, and is the reason why not only poetry, but an understanding of the nature of poetry and of the poetic element that is present in all meaningful language, is of vital importance. When I wrote this book I admitted (Chapter VIII, 6) that it was open to criticism as being somewhat overloaded. I would now go a little further and agree that, besides attempting to deal explicitly with many topics which the title *Poetic Diction* hardly covers, I have sometimes, in the text, included too much under the headings of *poetry* and *poet*. The sort of goings-on, for instance, which I have supposed in the final paragraph of Chapter VI, might be something more, they would certainly be something other, than what could ever properly be called 'poetry'—towards the production of which a certain unconscious, daemonic element now seems to me to be indispensable. But I would plead in extenuation that it lies in the nature of poetry to be always straining towards a plenum of consciousness, and of knowledge, which (if achieved) would bring about its own destruction, that it is, as has been finely said, 'a ship that is wrecked on entering harbour'. But I suggest that there is another ground, too, on which a book of this nature on this subject can be justified.

When people study law nowadays it is usually because they intend to practise it, but in the universities of the Middle Ages that study was the normal prelude to philosophy and theology. I take this to have been because it made men more conscious of the process of logical thinking. 'Law', as Professor Maitland pointed out, was 'the point where life and logic met'. In the business of defining rights and fixing responsibilities, the human mind first applies—more externally, at a slower pace and in a realm of voluntary effort (all of which make its elusive operation easier to detect)—the logical faculty which it may afterwards use, instantaneously, in the process of philosophy or science. We can even imagine a medieval Coleridge bringing the two together under a single term and calling one of them 'primary logic' and the other 'secondary logic'.

In the second Appendix to this book I accused Locke of treating simple *ideas* as though they were bare *percepts*, whereas, in fact, the mind is never aware of an idea until the imagination has been at work on the bare material given by the senses, perceiving resemblance, that is, demanding unity, because it is itself a unity. We can go further than this; the mind can never even perceive an object, *as* an object, till the imagination has been at work combining the *disjecta membra* of unrelated percepts into that experienced unity which the word 'object' denotes. Hume, who explicitly claimed that the idea is the impression, but also sometimes spoke of impressions as being made upon us by 'objects,' seems never to have clearly realized this, though he is not wholly consistent and there are passages in the *Treatise*—especially those in which he introduces the word *imagination*—which sometimes suggest the contrary.

By Coleridge's time philosophy had moved further into the realm of psychology. He fully grasped the part played by imagination in constructing not only the fictions of poets, but also the ordinary physical world which we speak of 'perceiving', though in fact we half perceive (that is, receive through sense-impressions) and half create it.

The act of imagination, performed by every man at this level, he called 'primary', to distinguish it from the same act performed at a more sophisticated level in the production of poetry—'an echo of the former, co-existing with the conscious will, yet still . . . identical with the primary in the *kind* of its operation'—which he called the 'secondary' imagination. This primary function of the imagination—never fully systematized by Coleridge—has been admirably demonstrated by Mr. James in the early chapters of his book, *Scepticism and Poetry*, to which I have already alluded. I refer the reader to him and, respectfully adopting his arguments, quote here his conclusion that:

'The highest reaches of the imagination are of a piece with the simplest act of perception, and issue from the demand for unity which is the life of the imagination.'[1]

Science deals with the world which it perceives but, seeking more and more to penetrate the veil of naïve perception, progresses only towards the goal of nothing, because it still does not accept in practice (whatever it may admit theoretically) that the mind first creates what it perceives as objects, including the instruments which Science uses for that very penetration. It insists on dealing with 'data', but there shall no data be given, save the bare percept. The rest is imagination. Only by imagination therefore can the world be known. And what is needed is, not only that larger and larger telescopes and more and more sensitive calipers should be constructed, but that the human mind should become increasingly aware of its own creative activity.

The difficulty lies in the fact that, outside poetry and the arts, that activity proceeds at an unconscious level. It has to be dug for. I have said that in the business of law the logical faculty operates more externally, at a slower pace and in a realm of voluntary effort which makes its elusive operation easier to detect. This is also true of the

[1] *Scepticism and Poetry*, p. 144. To avoid misrepresentation, I should add that, after pointing out that the mechanical representation of natural process is 'an imaginative scheme', Mr. James nevertheless accepts it as a permanently necessary and desirable one in all realms of inquiry including biology and psychology. He holds, distinguishing his own position from Whitehead's, that 'there is no point at which the mechanistic imagination of science can stop', and, in effect, agrees with the Positivists in restricting the term *knowledge* to verifiable 'fact' (meaning thereby 'event').

business of poetry. But here the problem is, no longer to proceed from life to thought, but to start from thought and move from there back to life. If law is the point where life and logic meet, perception is the point where life and imagination meet. But the point is out of sight—though not out of mind. Consequently, if men are ever to grow aware of it, they must start, in this case, from the other, the more subjective end. And I maintain that, just as the study of law was once a valuable exercise for other purposes besides the practice of law, so today the study of poetry and of the poetic element in all meaningful language is a valuable exercise for other purposes than the practice or better enjoyment of poetry. The secondary imagination can be our pointer to the primary. I do not say it is the only pointer, the only exercise that can lead to the desired end, namely, awareness of the part played by the imagination in perception, and by the individualized imagination in knowledge. I say it is a valuable one. To write poetry, said Wordsworth, a man must 'loaf and invite his soul'. I say nothing of the ethics of loafing, but it is certain that a man cannot understand what poetry is without inviting the soul, or in the words of Locke already quoted, reflecting on what passes in his own mind. Empiricists who question the mind's existence should not logically refuse to try the experiment. The best way to convince yourself that there is a world of inner experience is to explore it.

This book attempts to show how reflection on the poetic in language can lead to the perception that it flows from two different sources, one of these being the nature of language itself, especially in its earlier stages, and the other the individualized imagination of a poet; and how this in its turn leads to an understanding of the evolution of human consciousness. Once this has been understood the linguistic analyst, who attempts to tackle the problem of meaning without looking at its history, appears in much the same pitiful perspective as the earlier eighteenth-century biologists, who attempted to tackle the variety of natural species as though there were no such thing as evolution. It is quite true that logical speech is tautologous and cannot add to the sum of meaning or of knowledge. But the historical function of logical method has not been, to add to the sum of knowledge. It has been to engender subjectivity—self-consciousness. Once this has been achieved, as in the West it has very largely been achieved, today, there is no more that logic can do. Self-consciousness is indeed a *sine qua non* of undreaming knowledge, but it is not knowledge, it is more like its opposite; and once it has been achieved, logic, as far as the business of knowing is concerned, is *functus officio*. Or rather its surviving function is, to prevent a relapse.

Failure to grasp this lies at the root of most of the nonsense that has been deduced from the principle of tautology. Although the fallacy is not always as transparent as in the quotation selected above from *The Concept of Mind*, it is always the same in essence. For the argument from tautology rejects a supposed claim on behalf of logic, which no one who understands the nature of logic would ever make. It is true that the propositions of logic are tautologies, and that a tautology is meaningless. It is not true that they can therefore be ignored. When, in the course of an argument, I affirm a tautology, I do not do so (as both Wittgenstein and Professor Ryle appear to suppose) with the mistaken idea that I am purveying meaning. I do so, because it is the only way left to me of bringing my opponent to his senses. It is shock-treatment, designed to show him that he has failed to reflect, and therefore failed to grasp the very nature of thinking; that he has, for the moment at least, abandoned his sovereign unity and ceased to function as a human being. I may hope by this means to call him back from the first step on the road to what George Orwell called *double-think*; it does not follow that I shall succeed, if he is on other grounds determined to go there. Nor can I possibly succeed if the impossibility of reflection be his chosen premiss.

Logic can make us more precisely aware of the meaning already implicit in words. But the meaning must first of all be there and, if it is there, it will always be found to have been deposited or imparted by the poetic activity. This also is pointed out in the footnote to page 111 which I quoted at the beginning of this Preface. 'Poetry', in fact, for the most part employs the sentence form, in common with prose, but the poetic, as such, does not handle terms; it makes them.

When individual man, having achieved self-consciousness, returns to the making of poetry, the secondary imagination is at work on the making (or, if you like, restoration) of meaning. And, as the secondary imagination makes meaning, so the primary imagination makes 'things'. There is no other thinghood. It follows, as a matter of course, that a philosophy, or scienti-philosophy—let us call it scientism—which has reached the stage of abolishing the 'thing', will go on to abolish the mind.

It is interesting that Hume himself, on the rare occasions

when he carries his own premisses to their logical conclusion, assigns much the same primary function to the imagination. 'We have no idea', he says, 'of power or agency separate from the mind and belonging to causes,' and he criticizes those half-way philosophers who transcend the naïve without going forward to the truth, because 'they have sufficient force of genius to free them from the vulgar error that there is a natural and perceivable connection betwixt the several sensible qualities and actions of matter, but not sufficient to keep them from seeking for this connection in matter or causes'. To perceive that 'things', that the world which is today 'given' in adult consciousness, is the construct of imagination is the first and necessary step towards a true, participant knowledge as distinct from the haphazard pull-and-push ignorance which claims in public the name of science and admits in private that it knows nothing; which, when it turns inward to the mind of the Knower, finds there a nothingness within, to match the nothingness without. Hume taught us that the world of things is, in fact, a habit of mind. Russell affirming that 'whatever can be known can be known by science', denies *a priori* the possibility of disturbing the habit. Reflection on the poetic activity teaches us that the same imagination which created that kind of habit can both disturb it and create new ones.

The purely empirical knowledge which in our time has arrogated to itself the name of *science*, treats nature as an invading army treats an occupied country, mixing as little as possible with the inhabitants. We see it, in our own time, beginning to learn the lesson that you can do anything with bayonets except sit on them. Participant knowledge is a very different matter. But what is participant knowledge? In my parable of the motor-car called the universe the passengers should really themselves have been represented as little motor-cars, each having its own engine, and yet propelled, together with their carrier, by one and the same engine. But all such analogies break down. I have tried to indicate the answer in this book. Certainly it is only by the pursuit and application of such knowledge that man can hope to live in harmony with nature, as distinct from riding—and being ridden—roughshod. And so to live is, *ex hypothesi* (if Hume was right), to live in harmony with the unconscious depths of his own being.

Goethe gave more attention to botany, zoology and scientific method than he did to poetry. The pursuit of poetry seemed less important to him than the task of establishing the epistemological status of a conscious control of the primary imagination. I am convinced that he succeeded. The *Urphänomen* of his *Metamorphosenlehre* is the primary imagination voluntarily applied to perception (as the secondary imagination is voluntarily applied to ideas in the composition of poetry) and grasping the reality of nature by participation. In the years that have elapsed since this book was written a few thinkers and experimentalists, applying the Goethean method, have made notable advances in agriculture, medicine and elsewhere. I believe that the future of natural science is very largely in their hands.

But meanwhile what of poetry itself? The same period has produced, in England, some deeply felt and originally expressed work. But England has not seen during that period—nor indeed since the days of the Romantic Movement—any conjunction of poetic ability of the first class with a penetrating intellect equal to that of Coleridge or Keats; I mean the Keats promised by the Letters. And this is doubly unfortunate for the following reason. Apart from pleasurable entertainment (which must never be forgotten), there are two important functions which poetry is there to perform. One of them is the one I have stressed throughout this book, namely the making of meaning, which gives life to language and makes true knowledge possible. And this it does inasmuch as it is the vehicle of imagination. The other, lying much nearer the surface of life, is to mirror, not necessarily by approving, the characteristic response of the age in which it is written. Now it may happen, and it has been happening increasingly since the eighteenth century, that these two functions conflict. They may even be diametrically opposed to one another. For there may be an age of which the characteristic response is to deny the validity of imagination. And if that happens, a true and sensitive poet will find himself in a dilemma.

If anyone were inclined to doubt that ours is such an age, the degree of acceptance which the admittedly able and informed critical writings of Dr. I. A. Richards have won for themselves should be enough to satisfy him to the contrary. For in *The Principles of Literary Criticism*[1], *Coleridge on Imagination*,[2] and elsewhere Dr. Richards has sought no less than to define imagination in terms of a philosophy of Behaviourism—when it is precisely the fact of imagination which makes Behaviourism at once untrue and dangerous. Behaviourism was an attempt to carry to its logical conclusion in psychology the scientism

[1] Kegan Paul, 1925. [2] Kegan Paul, 1934

which natural science had come to take for granted, and which assumes that man is a detached observer of a world devoid of human spirit and 'going on by itself'. Within such a framework imagination can be no more than a kind of pretending, and it is as such that it is presented. The habits of mind to which Hume really reduced the objects of the external world have become so fixed and strong that the mind is now inclined to accept them as truths independent of itself—as some men will catalogue and study their own weaknesses as curiously and objectively as if they were another's. Our poets have not been much disposed to bother themselves with Hume and Coleridge and Goethe and all that. What they have done is to absorb, as it were through their pores, the findings of scientism and with them, the underlying attitude from which it partly springs and which it in part begets. Accordingly they have presented us with the human spirit as bewildered observer, or as agonized patient, compassionate in Hardy, humbled or repentant in Eliot, but always the observer, always the patient, helpless to alter anything but his own pin-pointed subjective emotion. No doubt the experience of the outside world as something 'which goes on by itself', and appears to have lost all connection with human imagination, was burnt into many modern poets by the combined violence and passivity of trench warfare; and today the objectized nothing, which scientism supposes at the base of the phenomenal world, is taking shape as the spectre of nuclear fission and scientific warfare on a world-wide scale. Some 'habit of mind'! the empiricist may well object, with a chuckle; and it is no part of my case that push-and-pull empiricism is weak or ineffectual, only that it is, like other giants, ignorant. The possibility of man's avoiding self-destruction depends on his realizing before it is too late that what he let loose over Hiroshima, after fiddling with its exterior for three centuries like a mechanical toy, was the forces of his own unconscious mind.

This conflict, in our own day, between the two proper functions of poetry is admirably brought out by Mr. G. Rostrever Hamilton in his little book *The Tell-tale Article*.[1] Writing as a deep admirer of T. S. Eliot, he proceeds nevertheless from an examination of the form of the most widely-read modern English poetry to a criticism of its spirit. He points out how, in the word-structure of both Eliot and Auden, 'verbs play a minor part as compared with nouns and adjectival phrases', and 'the intransitive verb is in high ratio to the transitive, and the participle is worked hard'. In their work and that of their followers, language tends to lose its rhetorical and architectural structure; and he shows how, especially in Eliot, it is thus peculiarly adapted to the poet's purpose of holding the mirror up to 'a world of bits and pieces', . . . 'a feeble world falling apart in dissolution'. Thus, the measure of the success with which the second function is fulfilled, is the extent to which the first has been let go. To speak effectively as a passive and helpless observer of a disintegrated world, 'the sinews of speech have to be loosened and the native energy of the verb subdued', and the author, with all his admiration, finds himself obliged at last to affirm that Eliot 'has done serious damage in his poetry to the structure of the English language'.

[1] Heinemann, 1949.

A similar decline (on which Mr. Hamilton touches only slightly) may be observed in the use of imagery and metaphor. The true, imaginative metaphor, as I have tried to show in this book, expresses and may communicate participant knowledge. But the type of metaphor with which modern poets have had most success, or most *réclame* (it is too early to say which), seeks to convey vividly, and with a certain effect of *frisson*, the disjointed impressions made by the surface of life upon the senses and the surface of the mind. The passion, if any, that imparts a precarious unity is a passion of withdrawal and detachment, of disillusionment, or, as in Eliot's case, a deep experience of personal or vicarious repentance. Eliot, in fact, solves the problem by using metaphor as sparingly as possible. He prefers the average word—which is a dead metaphor. Well, a dead metaphor is at least not stale and detachment is better than a show of participation based on borrowed plumes.

All generalization about the poetry of a recent period is likely to be misleading and, in the eyes of posterity, may be comic. In order to make my point, I have been compelled to write as if there were no living English poet whose feeling for language is of a different order of intimacy and who is moved to write, not by some fresh angle of moral or social asperity, but because he has experienced, and longs to bless and further, the creative imagination latent within the word itself. This is not the whole story. But a Preface may be excused for not being a balanced critical survey.

The man who accords (as I have suggested) an indulgent objectivity to his own settled habits did not always do so.

There was a time when they had not yet frozen into rules—and then he still regarded himself as responsible, and thought he might do something to change them. Of such a nature was the Romantic revolt against the encroaching grip of scientism on the mind of Europe, when prophetic voices like those of Blake, Schiller, Coleridge, Wordsworth, were raised in warning. But, with the single exception of Goethe, the doctrine of imagination died where it was born, in the garden of art and literature, and to-day a practising psychologist like Jung knows, and perhaps feels, more of the strength and primary significance of man's imaginal and myth-making faculty than the average poet or critic. Yet it is my belief, and my experience, that down in the oubliette where she has, perhaps necessarily, for a time immured herself, English poetry is still very much alive, and I shall count myself well paid if these scanty, but I believe suggestive, pages contribute, in however slight a degree, to her re-emergence into the daylight of imagination.

One final word: the dedication of this book remains unchanged. But as the pen-name which was printed on the flyleaf was abandoned by its owner shortly after the first edition appeared, I have now substituted his true name, to which his publications in many varied fields have since lent so much distinction. I do this rather in the interests of accuracy than as claiming any reflected share in that distinction, but I also grasp with both hands so opportune an occasion of rededicating this book in celebration of nearly half a lifetime's priceless friendship.

OWEN BARFIELD

February 1951

καὶ ἔστιν ὁ μὲν τοιοῦτος νοῦς τῷ πάντα γίνεσθαι, ὁ δὲ τῷ πάντα ποιεῖν . . . . καὶ οὗτος ὁ νοῦς χωριστὸς καὶ ἀμιγὴς καὶ ἀπαθής, τῇ οὐσίᾳ ὢν ἐνεργείᾳ . . . . τὸ δ' αὐτό ἐστιν ἡ κατ' ἐνέργειαν ἐπιστήμη τῷ πράγματι . . . . οὐ μνημονεύομεν δὲ, ὅτι τοῦτο μὲν ἀπαθές, ὁ δὲ παθητικὸς νοῦς φθαρτός, καὶ ἄνευ τούτου οὐθὲν νοεῖ.

Aristotle: *De Anima*, III, 5

' . . . grant me a nature having two contrary forces, the one of which tends to expand infinitely, while the other strives to apprehend or *find* itself in this infinity, and I will cause the whole world of intelligences with the whole system of their representations to rise up before you.'

Coleridge: *Biographia Literaria*. Ch. XIII.

I

DEFINITION AND EXAMPLES

When words are selected and arranged in such a way that their meaning either arouses, or is obviously intended to arouse, aesthetic imagination, the result may be described as *poetic diction*. Imagination is recognizable as aesthetic, when it produces pleasure merely by its proper activity. Meaning includes the whole content of a word, or of a group of words arranged in a particular order, other than the actual *sounds* of which they are composed. Thus, this book is concerned with a realm of human experience in which such an expression as 'prophets old' may, and probably will, 'mean' something quite different from 'old prophets'.

If the question, what is poetry? has never been answered, everyone will agree at least thus far: that it is not merely so many waves in the air or ink-marks on a piece of paper —that it exists primarily in the world of consciousness. Language itself, we feel, only springs into being as it is uttered by men, or heard by men, or thought by men. Whatever poetry may be, then, it is something more than the signs or sounds by which it is conveyed.

So decisive is this rule that the same sounds and signs may easily be vehicles of poetry at this place and not in that, at this time and not at that, to this person and not to the other. To the author of the famous article in *Blackwood's*, none of the sounds and signs composing *Endymion* were a vehicle of poetry. To the writer of this book few of those which compose the introductory section of Browning's *Ring and the Book* are a vehicle of poetry. To John Robinson of Bethnal Green *Paradise Lost* is not a vehicle of poetry. This is elementary. But what I wish to emphasize is that, while we can blame or commiserate these individuals, as we choose, for not maintaining or cultivating, or for not having had the opportunity to cultivate and maintain, the requisite sensibility, it is, very strictly speaking, meaningless—unless by way of a forcible hyperbole—to accuse them of mistaking something that 'is' poetry for something that 'is not'. The question of whether or no I can call a given group of words 'poetry' is, in fact, immediately dependent on my own inner experiences; and in constructing a theory of poetic diction, it is from those experiences that I am obliged to start.

In view, however, of the predominantly personal direction taken by literary criticism during the last few decades, it may be well to point out here that to *start* from personal experience does not necessarily mean to finish with it. One may start from direct, personal, aesthetic experience without prejudice to the possibility of arriving in the end at some objective standards of criticism—standards which a young critic might set before himself as an aid to the eliminations of just those personal affections and associations—the accidents rather than the substance of poetry—which are always at hand to distort his judgement.

EXAMPLES

I

Thlee-piecee bamboo, two-piecee puff-puff, walk-along inside, no-can-see.

II

Up then crew the red, red, cock,
And up and crew the grey;
The eldest to the youngest said,
''Tis time we were away'.

The cock he hadna craw'd but once,
And clapped his wings at a',
When the eldest to the youngest said,
'Brother, we must awa'.'

'The cock doth craw, the day doth daw,
The channerin' worm doth chide;
Gin we be miss'd out o' our place,
A sair pain we maun bide.'

III

Love is a sickness full of woes,
All remedies refusing;
A plant that with most cutting grows,
Most barren with best using.
Why so?
More we enjoy it, more it dies;
If not enjoy'd, it sighing cries—
Heigh ho!

Love is a torment of the mind,
A tempest everlasting;
And Jove hath made it of a kind
Not well, nor full nor fasting.
Why so?
More we enjoy it, more it dies;
If not enjoy'd, it sighing cries—
Heigh ho!

IV

The inferior priestess, at her altar's side,
Trembling, begins the sacred rites of pride.
Unnumbered treasures ope at once, and here
The various offerings of the world appear;
From each she nicely culls with curious toil,
And decks the goddess with the glittering spoil.
This casket India's glowing gems unlocks,
And all Arabia breathes from yonder box.
The tortoise here and elephant unite,
Transform'd to combs, the speckled and the white.
Here files of pins extend their shining rows,
Puffs, powders, patches, Bibles, billets-doux.
Now awful Beauty puts on all its arms;
The fair each moment rises in her charms,
Repairs her smiles, awakens every grace,
And calls forth all the wonders of her face;
Sees by degrees a purer blush arise,
And keener lightnings quicken in her eyes.
The busy sylphs surround their darling care:
These set the head, and those divide the hair;
Some fold the sleeve, whilst others plait the gown;
And Betty's praised for labours not her own.

v (*a*)

My soul is an enchanted boat,
Which, like a sleeping swan, doth float
Upon the silver waves of thy sweet singing;
And thine doth like an angel sit
Beside a helm conducting it,
Whilst all the winds with melody are ringing. . . .

v (*b*)

What is your substance, whereof are you made,
That millions of strange shadows on you tend?
Since every one hath, every one, one shade,
And you, but one, can every shadow lend. . . .

VI

Behold now this vast city, a city of refuge, the mansion-house of liberty, encompassed and surrounded with his protection; the shop of war hath not there more anvils and hammers waking, to fashion out the plates and instruments of armed justice in defence of beleaguered truth, than there be pens and heads there, sitting by their studious lamps, musing, searching, revolving new notions and ideas wherewith to present, as with their homage and their fealty, the approaching Reformation; others as fast reading, trying all things, assenting to the force of reason and convincement.

What could a man require more from a nation so pliant and so prone to seek after knowledge? What wants there to such a towardly and pregnant soil, but wise and faithful labourers, to make a knowing people, a nation of prophets, of sages, and of worthies? We reckon more than five months yet to harvest;

there need not be five weeks; had we but eyes to lift up, the fields are white already.

I have transcribed above six separate groups of English words, all of which have been proved capable, in one case, of arousing aesthetic imagination. To begin with, I shall ignore the *difference* between the sensations which the various examples are able to arouse, in an attempt to fix any elements which they have in common. The first example is Pidgin English for a three-masted screw steamer with two funnels. I have added it to the rest, in the first place, because it appears to me to be indisputable that such primitive and semi-foreign expressions often have value as poetic diction, and, in the second place, because, that being so, their very baldness is a great advantage. Detached from all historical associations and poetic tradition, and yet affecting us in a manner which is qualitatively the same as that of explicitly 'poetic' diction, they present, as it were, the lowest common measure of our subject.

II

THE EFFECTS OF POETRY

PLEASURE AND KNOWLEDGE

[1]

In examples II to VI one of the most efficient causes of pleasure is—palpably—sound; the rhythm, the music, and the manner in which rhythm and music are wedded to sense. The sound of language is crucially relevant to its poetic meaning, indeed, owing to the peculiar relation of the vocal organs to the rest of the body, it is relevant even to those correspondences which will be considered later under the heading of 'metaphor'. It has a bearing, too, on the essentially *active* nature of the poetic consciousness, which is one of the findings of this book. But the subject is an extremely subtle and delicate one and, thanks to the changes of form which words undergo in the course of their history, is particularly difficult to discuss theoretically and illustrate with examples. Though they may be indistinguishable in practice, topically it is possible to distinguish the intellectual element in poetic meaning from the tonal; and where there is more than one topic, it is reasonable to deal with one at a time. Accordingly I have, for the purpose of this book, considered sound as lying outside the province of poetic diction, properly so called, and it will not be further discussed.

[2]

When I try to describe in more detail than by the phrase 'aesthetic imagination' what experience it is to which at some time or other I have been led, and at any time may be led again, by all of these examples, I find myself obliged to define it as a 'felt change of consciousness', where 'consciousness' embraces all my awareness of my surroundings at any given moment, and 'surroundings' includes my own feelings. By 'felt' I mean to signify that the change itself is noticed, or attended to. To take the simplest example: No. 1:—when I, as European adult, actually observe or visualize a three-masted screw steamer with two funnels, the manner in which I immediately experience my surroundings, the *meaning* which they have for me, is determined by the various concepts which *I* have learnt, since my childhood, to unite with the percept, or complex of percepts, underlying the phenomenon in question. By 'percept' I mean that element in my experience, which in no way depends on my own mental activity, present or past—the pure sense-datum. The concepts likely to be operative in this case are reflected in such English words as 'mast', 'mechanical propulsion', 'steam', 'coal', 'smoke', 'chimney for smoke to escape by', etc., all of which are summed up and, as it were, fused in my own peculiar and habitual idea of 'steamer'.

It is this idea which determines for me the quality, or meaning, of my immediate experience in observation.

Now when I read the words 'thlee-piecee bamboo, two-piecee puff-puff, walk-along-inside, no-can-see', I am for a moment transported into a totally different kind of consciousness. I see the steamer, not through my own eyes, but through the eyes of a primitive South-Sea Islander. His experience, his *meaning*, is quite different from mine, for it is the product of quite different concepts. This he reveals by his choice of words; and the result is that, for a moment, I shed Western civilization like an old garment and behold my steamer in a new and strange light.

[3]

Without reducing our definition of poetic diction to an absurdity, we can hardly maintain that this particular example (No 1) would be 'poetic' to the South-Sea Islanders themselves. On the contrary, we may safely suppose it to be felt there as a part of the business jargon of every day.[1] It is thus a particularly clear-cut example of the fact, referred to in Chapter I, that a given group of words may be a vehicle of poetry to one individual, or group of individuals, and not to another. It may, for instance, be unpoetic to the consciousness which originates it, but poetic to the consciousness which receives or contemplates it. This is an aspect of poetic diction to which I shall have to return later.

From this it follows that the extent to which the selec-

[1] *Pidgin* is in fact said to be the Chinese version of the English word 'business'.

tion and arrangement of words is due to a consciously creative effort ('art') on the part of some one human being ('poet') varies as between the six examples. The range of variation must probably remain a matter of dispute; but it would be at any rate arguable that it is from nought in the first example up to eighty or ninety per cent in the last two. Obviously this percentage can never rise to a hundred, because even the most original poet is obliged to work with words, and words, unlike marble or pigment or vibrations in the air, owe their very substance ('meaning') to the generations of human beings who have previously used them. No poet, therefore, can be the creator of all the meaning in his poem.

The point will be made plainer by taking an intermediate example. Consider No. II. There is no need to enter into the old question of the 'communal origin' of ballads; for however pronounced may be the stamp of individual genius in the best English ballads, it still remains indisputable that they have in common certain turns of expression, certain tricks of metre and repetition and narrative and that, while on the one hand these cannot all be due to the genius of one single man, on the other hand, they do undoubtedly contribute to the poetic quality of the diction of the ballad. Thus, if I wish to be especially critical, I can divide my enjoyment of a ballad into two parts: I enjoy it as ballad, and I enjoy it as poem. This fact comes out very clearly if I read a great number of ballads one after the other. For then, in time, the 'ballad' quality ceases to arouse my aesthetic imagination at all, and I depend wholly on the individual quality of the one particular example I am reading at the moment.

So, too, in the lyric from Campion (No. III):—part of my æsthetic experience I owe to the individual genius of the poet Campion. Part, on the other hand—and I believe anyone who seriously examines his feelings will reach the same conclusion—is due to something which I will call its 'Elizabethan-ness'. Needless to say, the phenomenon is not peculiar to the Elizabethan lyric. It is true of other times and places, of the poetry of the Greek Anthology, for example, of the French Pléiade, of the English Metaphysicals, or the Cavalier lyric, and it has been well named by some critic 'joint-stock poetry'. It arises wherever different poets work together in a kind of coterie or come under the same contemporary influence; in the lyric it is brought out especially strongly when we hear the words set to the music of contemporary composers. And it is always true that if I read or hear too much, if I saturate my imagination with poetry of the same genre, I lose my power to appreciate is *as* genre, and am thrown back on the achievement, such as it may be, of the individual poet.

In such cases, then, we distinguish two separate causes of poetic pleasure; and we are enabled to do this because the realization and contemplation of this 'joint-stock' element is itself a third pleasure. It might be compared with the delight which Chaucer took in contemplating 'the law of kind'. Further, our enjoyment of this 'joint-stock' element is something in which the producers of the diction in question can have had no share. This was a part of their work, of which they were unconscious, for they were actually *living* it.

[4]

Thus, an introspective analysis of my experience obliges me to say that appreciation of poetry involves a 'felt change of consciousness'. The phrase must be taken with some exactness. Appreciation takes place at the actual moment of change. It is not simply that the poet enables me to see with his eyes, and so to apprehend a larger and fuller world. He may indeed do this, as we shall see later; but the actual moment of the pleasure of appreciation depends upon something rarer and more transitory. It depends on the change itself. If I pass a coil of wire between the poles of a magnet, I generate in it an electric current—but I only do so while the coil is positively moving across the lines of force. I may leave the coil at rest between the two poles and in such a position that it is thoroughly permeated by the magnetic field; but in that case no current will flow along the conductor. Current only flows when I am actually bringing the coil in or taking it away again. So it is with the poetic mood, which, like the dreams to which it has so often been compared, is kindled by the passage from one plane of consciousness to another. It lives during that moment of transition and then dies, and if it is to be repeated, some means must be found of renewing the transition itself.

Poetry, as a possession, as our own souls enriched, is another matter. But when it has entered as deeply as that into our being, we no longer concern ourselves with its *diction*. At this stage the diction has served its end and may be forgotten. For, if ever we go back to linger lovingly over the exquisite phrasing of some fragment of poesy whose essence has long been our own, and of which the spirit has become a part of our every waking moment, if we do this, is it not *for the very reason* that we want to renew the thrill which accompanied the first acquisition of the treasure? As our lips murmur the well-known—or it may be the long-forgotten—words, we are trying, whether deliberately or no, to cast ourselves back into the frame of mind which was ours before we had learnt the lesson. Why? Because we know instinctively that, if we are to feel pleasure, we must have change. Everlasting day can no more freshen the earth with dew than everlasting night, but the change from night to day and from day back again to night.

That we are not always successful in the wistful quest is matter of only too common experience. Mr. Santayana has expressed with great beauty this sometimes overlooked fact of the rareness of real aesthetic experience:

'Men are habitually insensible to beauty. Tomes of aesthetic criticism hang on a few moments of real delight and intuition. It is in rare and scattered instants that beauty smiles even on her adorers, who are reduced for habitual comfort to remembering her past favours. An aesthetic glow may pervade experience, but that circumstance is seldom remarked; it figures only as an influence working subterraneously on thoughts and judgements which in themselves take a cognitive or practical direction. Only when the aesthetic ingredient becomes predominant do we exclaim, How beautiful! Ordinarily the pleasures which formal perception gives remain an undistinguished part of our comfort or curiosity.

'Taste is formed in those moments when aesthetic

emotion is massive and distinct; preferences then grow conscious, judgements then put into words will reverberate through calmer hours; they will constitute prejudices, habits of apperception, secret standards for all other beauties. A period of life in which such intuitions have been frequent may amass tastes and ideals sufficient for the rest of our days. Youth in these matters governs maturity, and while men may develop their early impressions more systematically and find confirmations of them in various quarters, they will seldom look at the world afresh or use new categories in deciphering it. Half our standards come from our first masters, and the other half from our first loves. Never being so deeply stirred again, we remain persuaded that no objects save those we then discovered can have a true sublimity. . . . Thus the volume and intensity of some appreciations, especially when nothing of the kind has preceded, makes them authoritative over our subsequent judgements. On those warm moments hang all our cold systematic opinions; and while the latter fill our days and shape our careers it is only the former that are crucial and alive.'

Is there anybody so fortunate as to be able to dispute the truth in this passage? Yet that precarious element in poetry, which has puzzled critics and poets alike, may at any rate become clearer to us, may even come a little more under our control, if once we can elucidate its causes. And to me the principal cause appears to be that poetic experience depends on a 'difference of potential', a kind of *discrepancy* between two moods or modes of consciousness. It is from this point, I take it, that a profitable study of the *psychology* of aesthetics would diverge.

[5]

At the end of the last section a distinction was drawn between poetry as the cause of immediate pleasure (the subject of the three preceding sections) and 'poetry as a possession'. What, then, is meant by poetry as a possession? To some extent in all the examples, but especially in No. V, I am impressed not merely by the *difference* between my consciousness and the consciousness of which they are the expression, but by something more. I find that, in addition to the moment or moments of aesthetic pleasure in appreciation, I gain from them a more permanent boon. It is as though my own consciousness had actually been expanded. In V(*a*), for example, the image contains so much truth and beauty that henceforth the eyes with which I behold real boats and waves and swans, the ears with which in the right mood I listen to a song, are actually somehwhat different.

Now my normal everyday experience, as human being, of the world around me depends entirely on what *I* bring to the sense-datum from within; and the absorption of this metaphor into my imagination has enabled me to bring more than I could before. It has created something in me, a faculty or a part of a faculty, enabling me to observe what I could not hitherto observe. This ability to recognize significant resemblances and analogies, considered as in action, I shall call *knowledge*; considered as a *state*, and apart from the effort by which it is imparted and acquired, I shall call it *wisdom*. The elements in poetic diction which must conduce to it are, as we shall see, metaphor and simile. The use of the word 'significant' will be justified in due course.

A little reflection shows that all *meaning*—even of the most primitive kind—is dependent on the possession of some measure of this power. Where it was wholly absent, the entire phenomenal cosmos must be extinguished. All sounds would fuse into one meaningless roar, all sights into one chaotic panorama, amid which no individual objects—not even colour itself—would be distinguishable. Let the reader imagine for a moment that he is standing in the midst of a normal and familiar environment—houses, trees, grass, sky, etc.—when, suddenly, he is deprived by some supernatural stroke of every vestige of memory—and not only of memory, but also of all those assimilated, forgotten experiences, which comprise his power of *recognition*. He is asked to assume that, in spite of this, he still retains the full measure of his cognitive faculty as an adult. It will appear, I think, that for the first few moments his consciousness—if it can bear that name—will be deprived not merely of all thought, but even of all perception, as we ordinarily understand the word[1]—unless we choose to suppose a certain unimaginable minimum, a kind of panorama of various light, which he will confront with a vacant and uncomprehending stare. It is not merely that he will be unable to realize that that square, red and white object is a 'house', and to form concepts of an inside with walls and ceilings—he will not even be able to see it *as* a square, red and white object. For the most elementary distinctions of form and colour are only apprehended by us with the help of the concepts

[1] Here, however, called *observation*, *perception* being reserved for that element in our 'reading' of the world, which is entirely independent of the understanding.

which we have come to unite with the pure sense-datum. And these concepts we acquire and fix, as we grow up, with the help of words—such words as *square*, *red*, etc. On the basis of past perceptions, using language as a kind of storehouse,[1] we gradually build up our ideas, and it is only these (cf. II, 2) which enable us to become 'conscious', as human beings, of the world around us. There is, therefore, nothing pretentious or dilettante in describing my experience as 'an expansion of consciousness'.

[6]

While this expansion (*knowledge*) may remain as something of a permanent possession (*wisdom*), my aesthetic *pleasure* will still, in the case under review, only accompany the actual *moment* of expansion, as it before accompanied the moment of change. In fact, as far as the possibility of aesthetic *pleasure* is concerned, expansion is merely one particular form taken by the necessary change, or movement; and if I wish to repeat the pleasure, I am obliged, as was pointed out (§ 4), to throw myself back into the imaginative content which was mine before I had made these metaphors a part of my meaning of life.

To trace out this alternating basis of the poetic mood into further detail, and to strip it of some of its obscurity,

[1] The *exact* relations of cause and effect between language and thought need not be discussed. Nor need we at present consider whether the two are indeed absolutely inseparable, as e.g. Locke and Max Müller held. It is enough that for the *communication* of thought, and of the feelings which thoughts can arouse, and for the storing and public record of them, language *is*, in fact, the common medium.

it will be necessary to consider first of all the nature and history of language itself. Incidentally, this is quite in accord with the traditions of the subject. Dante felt obliged to write at length on the subject of language. And if he, like the Frenchman Du Bellay after him, still regarded it rather from a national point of view, Wordsworth and Shelley showed, in a later age, how a proper study of poetic diction is inseparable from the study of language as a whole.

'In the infancy of society [wrote Shelley] every author is necessarily a poet, because language itself is poetry. . . . Every original language near to its source is itself the chaos of a cyclic poem.'[1]

And Wordsworth insisted that the subject 'could not be determined without pointing out in what manner language and the human mind act and react on eath other, and without retracing the revolutions, not of literature alone, but likewise of society itself.'[2]

'Poetry', said Coleridge, 'is the best words in the best order;' in other words, it is 'the best language.' By considering it as such, I hope to mark out a sheet on which it would be possible to plot, to some purpose, the lesser vagaries of English versification. Without some such ground-plan all criticism, all theorizing on the problems of poetic diction, all speculation as to what was or was not beautiful or justifiable in the poetry of the past, and, above all, all attempts to apply such theories to the poetry of the present, must peter out in expressions of personal taste. If my inclination is to scepticism and polite society, I shall exalt Pope and Racine at the expense of Dante and

[1] *A Defence of Poetry*.

[2] Appendix on the phrase '*Poetic Diction*'.

Shelley; if to natural scenery and creative evolution, I shall praise Wordsworth and spit upon Waller. It does not seem unduly arrogant to suggest that criticism is tired of this cat and dog business and needs a little fresh air.

III

METAPHOR

[1]

In the West, since Plato's time, the study of language has been developed mainly by grammarians and logicians. It is true that about a hundred and fifty years ago a more historical conception of philology suddenly began to spread rapidly over Europe. But the emphasis was still, until recently, on the external *forms* of words. The result is, as far as I am aware, that no really profound study has yet been made of *meaning*—that is to say, of the meanings of individual words. This subject—Semantics, as it is now commonly called—makes its first, embryonic appearance as a cautionary chapter following the chapter on Terms in a logical textbook, and it is not until long after that it acquires a separate existence, and even a hint of wings, in the work of writers like Archbishop Trench, Max Müller, and, today, Mr. Pearsall Smith.

The extraordinarily intimate connection between, language and thought (the Greek word λόγος combined, as we should say, both meanings) might lead one to expect that the philosophers at least would have turned their attention to the subject long ago. And so, indeed, they did, but with a curiously disproportionate amount of interest. The cause of this deficiency is, I think, to be found in the fact that Western philosophy, from Aristotle onwards, is itself a kind of offspring of Logic. To anyone attempting to construct a metaphysic in strict accordance with the canons and categories of formal Logic, the fact that the meanings of words change, not only from age to age, but from context to context, is certainly interesting; but it is interesting solely because it is a nuisance.

I will try to make this clearer by a comparison. The financial mysteries of 'inflation' and 'deflation' may likewise be said to 'interest' the practising merchant. But that interest is, for the most part, of a limited sort. Since money is the very basis of all his operations, he has, I think it can be said, an instinctive distaste for the mere possibility that money-units themselves should be found to have only an arbitrary 'subjective' value—that they should prove to be simply cross-sections of an endless process taking place in time. If that is true, all is lost. The dykes are opened. Like magic, he sees shrewd practical maxims turning into rarified academic theories, and a comparatively simple and intelligible system of ackowledged *facts* ('the economic verities') having to be rigged with all sorts of super-subtle reservations and *ceteris paribus's*, before it will bear the faintest relation to contemporary realities.

What money is to the conservative economist, words are to the conservative philosopher. For the conception of money as a 'symbol of barter' and the conception of words as the 'names of things' are, both alike, not so much untrue as 'out of date'; and for the same reason: not because the advance of science has revealed avoidable ancient errors, but because the facts themselves have changed. Once upon a time money really was an immediate substitute for barter, and once upon a time words could really be the expression on the face of concrete reality. Error—or, at best, waste of energy—is in both cases the fruit of unwillingness to recognize essential change. The spell of the immediate past proves too strong; and, just as the stubborn economist, with his eyes fixed on that past, turns his back on all new-fangled nonsense and nails his colours stoutly to the mast of *stabilization*, so the philosopher waves aside the study of meaning and still maintains a desperate faith in the ancient system of *definitions*. In both instances, it may be that somewhere—deep down in the unconscious—a voice has cried *Lass mich schlafen*!

Whatever the cause, nearly all that has hitherto been said on the semantic aspect of language has been said from one point of view only. And from that point of view it has been said wonderfully well. The original twist was given by the Father of Logic himself, when he included in his *Organon* a brief treatise *De Interpretatione*, and since then the conception of language as the prime material of logical constructions has been developed many times with infinite delicacy. It is difficult, for example, to praise too highly the limpid clarity of the third book of Locke's *Essay on the Human Understanding*; and even as recently as the last century Mr. Bosanquet found memorable things to say in the opening chapters of his *Logic*. It may be that other modern philosophers have done as well, or better.

We have had, then, to the full, language as it is grasped

by logical mind. What we have not had—or what we have only had in hints and flashes—is language as it is grasped by poetic mind. The fundamental difference between logical and poetic mind (which has very little to do with the fashionable contrast between Poetry and Science) will appear farther in the course of this book, wherein I have myself attempted to sketch the way in which a poetic understanding would approach the problem. I have, however, made no attempt to write what I should so much like to see written—a true, poetic history and philosophy of language. On the contrary, it has been my object to avoid (except perhaps in two of the Appendices) entering deeper into the nature of language than is absolutely necessary, in order to throw on 'Poetry', in the usual literary sense of that word, the kind of light which, I think, needs to be thrown.

[2]

The most conspicuous point of contact between meaning and poetry is *metaphor*. For one of the first things that a student of etymology—even quite an amateur student—discovers for himself is that every modern language, with its thousands of abstract terms and its nuances of meaning and association, is *apparently* nothing, from beginning to end, but an unconscionable tissue of dead, or petrified, metaphors. If we trace the meanings of a great many words—or those of the elements of which they are composed—about as far back as etymology can take us, we are at once made to realize that an overwhelming proportion, if not all, of them referred in earlier days to one of these two things—a solid, sensible object, or some animal (probably human) activity. Examples abound on every page of the dictionary. Thus, an apparently objective scientific term like *elasticity*, on the one hand, and the metaphysical *abstract*, on the other, are both traceable to verbs meaning 'draw' or 'drag'. *Centrifugal* and *cetripetal* are composed of a noun meaning 'a goad' and verbs signifying 'to flee' and 'to seek' respectively; *epithet*, *theme*, *thesis*, *anathema*, *hypothesis*, etc., go back to a Greek verb, 'to put', and even *right* and *wrong*, it seems, once had the meanings of 'stretched' and so 'straight' and 'wringing' or 'sour'. Some philologists, looking still further back into the past, have resolved these two classes into one, but this is immaterial to the point at issue.

'Nihil in intellectu', wrote Locke, 'quod non prius fuerit in sensu.' And Anatole France, in his *Jardin d'Épicure* has adorned this theory of thought with a characteristically modern jumble of biological, anthropological, and etymological ideas:

'Et qu'est-ce-que penser ? Et comment pense-t-on ? Nous pensons avec des mots; cela seul est sensuel et ramène à la nature. Songez-y, un metaphysicien n'a pour constituer le système du monde, que le cri perfectionné des singes et des chiens. Ce qu'il appelle spéculation profonde et méthode transcendante, c'est de mettre bout à bout, dans un ordre arbitraire, les onomatopées qui criaient la faim, la peur et l'amour dans les forêts primitives, et auxquelles se sont attachées peu à peu des significations qu'on croit abstraites quand elles sont seulement relachées.

'N'ayez pas peur que cette suite de petits cris éteints et affaiblis qui composent un livre de philosophie nous en apprenne trop sur l'univers pour que nous ne puissions plus y vivre. Dans la nuit où nous sommes tous, le savant se cogne au mur, tandis que l'ignorant reste tranquillement au milieu de la chambre.'

Later on, in an imaginary dialogue between a metaphysician and an etymologist, the latter kindly offers to resolve into its elements the sentence 'L'âme possède Dieu dans la mesure où elle participe de l'absolu'. When he has finished with it, it reads: 'Le souffle est assis sur celui qui brille, au boisseau du don qu'il reçoit en ce qui est tout délié'.

[3]

Anatole France's etymologist, then, sees language as beginning with simple, purely perceptual meanings, and building up, by metaphor, a series of meanings which pretend to be 'abstract,' when they are really only vague. Now it will at once be seen that the conception of the primitive mind, on which this imagination is based, would make it correspond exactly with the state of consciousness into which the reader was asked to throw himself (II, 5) as the result of a fictitious 'stroke'. So that the process by which the words mentioned above have acquired the meanings which they now possess would, on this view, be identical with the process by which Shelley was able to write:

My soul is an enchanted boat . . . (Ex. V).

To carry the illustration further: should the feeling and idea which these lines embody ever become sufficiently well-known and widespread, one can easily perceive how in a few hundred, or in a few thousand years, the word *boat*, or perhaps the phrase *enchanted boat* might lose its present meaning and call up to the minds of our posterity, not a vessel, but the concept 'soul' as enriched by Shelley's imagination. A new word, abridged perhaps to something like *chambote*, might grow into being. Language actually abounds, as we shall see, in meanings, and is not lacking in words, which have come into it in just this way.

We are tempted to infer that, as language grows older, it must *necessarily* become richer and richer as poetic material; it must become intrinsically more and more poetic. The bald sentence: 'Le souffle est assis sur celui qui brille, au boisseau du don qu'il reçoit en ce qui est tout délié', is palpably prosaic, and its original can only begin to arouse imagination and feeling at whatever point in time *âme* begins to add to its material meaning a vague suggestion of 'something like breath indeed, but more living, sentient, inward—a part of my Self', and *Dieu* to acquire the signification of 'something like sky, yet more living, corresponding, therefore, to something in me'. Thus, from the primitive meanings assumed by the etymologist, we are led to fancy metaphor after metaphor sprouting forth and solidifying into new meanings—vague, indeed, yet evocative of more and more subtle echoes and reactions. From being mere labels for material objects, words gradually turn into magical charms. Out of a catalogue of material facts is developed—thanks to the efforts of forgotten primitive geniuses—all that we know today as 'poetry'.

Was it really like this? To have observed a resemblance

between, say, a straight stick and an inner feeling, and to have used the name of the stick to describe the feeling is indeed to have made a long step forward. From now onward—so we perhaps imagine—upon the chaotic darkness in which it first awoke, human consciousness begins to cast its own brilliant and increasing light. It flings its beams further and further into the night. 'With the beginning of language', writes Ludwig Noiré, a disciple of Max Müller, 'the period of spiritual creation began; the light glimmered feebly and inconspicuously at first which now illumines heaven and earth with its rays—the divine light of reason . . .' and he adds, still more enthusiastically:

'the first step is herewith hewn, by the joint toil of reason and speech, in the hard rock, where a second and then others must follow, till aeons hence the lofty summit is reached, and reason enthroned on high sees all the world beneath as the theatre where her might and glory is displayed, and ventures forth upon new flights through the unexplored realms of heaven not even here without a clue, any more than at the hour of her birth, afforded by her own—but now purely ideal—constructions.'

And Shelley: 'Metaphorical language marks the before unapprehended relations of things and perpetuates their apprehension until words, which represent them, become, through time, signs for portions or classes of thought, instead of pictures of integral thoughts.'

Here again we seem to have a picture of language becoming, intrinsically, more and more poetic; for who could make poetry out of a disjointed list of unrelated percepts? And what is the very essence of poetry if it is not this 'metaphorical language'—this marking of the before unapprehended relations of things?

[4]

Yes, but is it poetry, or reason that is being exalted? Shelley, in the passage just quoted, seems hardly to distinguish the one from the other. Let us actually examine the sentiments of those who have thought historically, not on language, but on poetry itself. 'As civilization advances', said Macaulay, 'poetry almost necessarily declines.' Peacock's *Four Ages of Poetry*, notwithstanding its irony at the expense of 'progress', is a genuine dirge on the gradual murder of the Muse by that very Reason, whose 'divine light' the philologist was constrained to hymn. Mr. Courthope, in his *Liberal Movement in English Literature*, qualifies a similar opinion by the subtle distinction: 'As civilization advances, the matter for poetic creation diminishes, while the powers of poetic expression are multiplied'. And even to Shelley, who wrote with the express purpose of refuting Peacock, it is in 'the infancy' of society that 'every author is a poet, because language itself is poetry'. There is no need to go further for examples. They are found everywhere. Thus the general view is the exact opposite of what one would be led to expect. Indeed, nothing in the world seems so likely to turn a man into a *laudator temporis acti* as an historical survey of poetry. Even today it remains a moot point among the critics whether the very first extant poet of our Western civilization has ever been surpassed for the grandeur and sublimity of his diction.

Yet if language had indeed advanced, by continual accretion of metaphor, from roots of speech with the simplest material reference, to the complex organism which we know today, it would surely be *today* that every author is a poet—today, when a man cannot utter a dozen words without wielding the creations of a hundred named and nameless poets. Given the necessary consciousness of this (i.e. an historical knowledge of, and feeling for, language),[1] our pleasure in such a sentence as—for example—'I simply love that idea' should be infinitely more sublime than our pleasure—as far as the language itself is concerned—in reading Homer. How is it then that, in actual fact, we find this almost universal consciousness that the golden age of poetry is in the *infancy* of society? Bearing in mind our conclusion that *pleasure* in poetic diction depends on the difference between two planes or levels of consciousness, we can indeed see why language, at an early stage, should delight us. But what follows? If this theory of the growth of language, by means of metaphor, from simple perceptual meanings to complex psychic ones is a correct theory, it follows that our pleasure in such relatively primitive diction ought to be of a poor and unsatisfying nature, compared to our pleasure in the diction of a modern writer who wields these wonderful meanings. It should be more akin to the pleasure we take in such primitive locutions as Example I, where the change of consciousness is effected by contraction rather than expansion—as for example,

[1] Language reserves one satisfaction for the observer, all the more lively because it is not sought after: the satisfaction, namely, of feeling a metaphor, whose value has not hitherto been understood, suddenly open and reveal itself. Bréal; *Semantics*, p. 129.

by emphasizing those purely external, pictorial relations of things, which sophistication—saving the painter's case—too often induces us to ignore. Is this true? We know at once that it is not. We know from first-hand experience that resemblances between the Greek poetry of Homer's day, or even the Anglo-Saxon of the author of *Beowulf*'s, and, say, pidgin-English—though tell-tale—are yet in point of value so slight as to be almost negligible. We find, in fact, that this old poetry has the knowledge-value, as well as the pleasure-value, and has it in a high degree.

Now, to the genuine critic, the spiritual fact of his own aesthetic experience, when once he knows inwardly that it is purged of all personal affection,[1] must have at least equal weight with any reported historical or scientific facts which may be placed beside it. Beyond that, it must be his aim, as it is the aim of all knowledge, to reconcile or relate conceptually all the elements included in his perceptual experience; among this latter he must number his own aesthetic reactions.

[5]

Since, then, ancient poetry is simply ancient language at its best (II, 6), we must now try and discover why it is that this best ancient language, when it is compared with the best modern language, so often appears, not simply as naïve, but, on the contrary, as endued with an extra-

[1] That is to say, when he knows that his pleasure arises from the *proper activity* of imagination (I, 1) and not from any incidental suggestion of pleasurable sensation—in the case of metaphor, when it is the pure *content* of the image, and not only the *reference*, which delights.

ordinary richness and splendour. Where, we must ask, is the fallacy in that proud conception of the evolution of language from simplicity and darkness to complexity and light?

It should be remembered that we are here dealing, not with 'poetry', which includes the creative activity itself, but with 'poetic diction'—that is to say, with the language of poetic compositions, as we actually find them written in different ages. Someone might come forward and say: But this is nonsense. You are leaving out of account the one thing that really matters and making a mystery of what is left. When people say that Homer has never been surpassed, they mean precisely what they say—that he has never been surpassed. His poetry is sublime because he himself was sublime, and if there has been no such great poetry since, it is because there has been no such great man; or, at any rate, if such a man has lived, he cannot have turned his attention to poetry.

The reply to such an objection would be threefold: (i) It has already been pointed out that there are certain elements in poetic diction which are clearly *not* traceable to any identifiable individual. (ii) Homer is in any case a bad example to choose, as his individual existence is disputed. (iii) This problem of the responsibilityof individuals for poetic value is just one of the most important questions which a theory of poetic diction has to attack. To make any assumptions beforehand would be to beg it. The only way to start with an unprejudiced mind is to take actual examples of poetic diction (see definition, I. 1) and to work backward from them to their sources. This method does not exclude the possibility of arriving *eventually* at the conclusion expressed in the objection—that the poetic element in language is, and always has been, the result of individual effort, but we have certainly not arrived at that conclusion yet. The question will come up for discussion, in fact, in its proper place.

A hundred and fifty years ago Dr. Hugh Blair wrote in his *Lectures on Rhetoric*:

'We are apt, upon a superficial view, to imagine that those modes of expression which are called Figures of Speech are among the chief refinements of Speech, not invented till after language had advanced to its late periods, and mankind were brought into a polished state; and that then they were devised by orators and rhetoricians. The contrary of this is the truth. Mankind never employed so many Figures of Speech, as when they had hardly any words for expressing their meaning.

'For, first, the want of proper names for every object, obliged them to use one name for many; and, of course, to express themselves by comparisons, metaphors, allusions and all those substituted forms of Speech, which render Language figurative. Next, as the objects with which they were most conversant, were the sensible, material objects around them, names would be given to these objects long before words were invented for signifying the dispositions of the mind, or any sort of moral and intellectual ideas. Hence, the early language of men being entirely made up of words descriptive of sensible objects, it became, of necessity, extremely metaphorical . . .'

Now this appears to be a conception of language which, since the time of Locke, has been held by most people who have troubled to write on the subject. Yet it proves (unless one stretches the meanings of such words as *metaphor* and *trope* intolerably far) to be quite unreasonable. For how is it arrived at? In this way: (i) The theorist beholds metaphors and similitudes being invented by poets and others in his own time. (ii) Examining the more recent history of language, he finds many examples of such metaphors having actually become a part of language, that is to say, having become meanings.[1] (iii) Delving deeper still into etymology, he discovers that all our words were at one time 'the names of sensible objects', and (iv) he jumps to the conclusion that they therefore, at that time, had *no other meaning*.[2] From these four observations he proceeds to deduce, fifthly, that the application of these names of sensible objects to what we now call *insensible* objects was deliberately 'metaphorical'.

In other words, although, when he moves backwards through the history of language, he finds it becoming more and more *figurative* with every step, yet he has no hesitation in assuming a period—still further back—when it was not figurative at all! To supply, therefore, the missing link in his chain of linguistic evolution, he proceeds to people the 'infancy of society' with an exalted race of amateur poets. Thus, Max Müller in his *Science of Language* speaks with confidence of the 'metaphorical period', describing how:

[1] So M. Bréal (*Semantics*): 'There is the same difference between the tropes of language and the metaphors of poets as between a product in common use and a recent conquest of science'. See also Chapters VII and VIII *post*.

[2] See Blair, quoted above: and compare Locke (*Human Understanding*, III, i. 5): '*Spirit*, in its primary signification, is breath, *angel* a messenger', etc., etc.

'*Spiritus* in Latin meant originally blowing, or wind. But when the principle of life within man or animal had to be named, its outward sign, namely the breath of the mouth, was naturally chosen to express it. Hence in Sanskrit asu, breath and life; in Latin *spiritus*, breath and life. Again, when it was perceived that there was something else to be named, not the mere animal life, but that which was supported by this animal life, the same word was chosen, in the modern Latin dialects, to express the spiritual as opposed to the mere material or animal element in man. All this is a metaphor.

'We read in the Veda, ii. 3, 4: "Who saw the first-born when he who had no form (lit. bones) bore him that had form? Where was the breath (asuh), the blood (asrik), the self (atma) of the earth? Who went to ask this from any that knew it?"

'Here breath, blood, self are so many attempts at expressing what we should now call "cause".'

It would be difficult to conceive anything more perverse than this paragraph; there is, indeed, something painful in the spectacle of so catholic and enthusiastic a scholar as Max Müller seated so firmly on the saddle of etymology, with his face set so earnestly towards the tail of the beast. He seems to have gone out of his way to seek for impossibly modern and abstract concepts to project into that luckless dustbin of pseudo-scientific fantasies—the mind of primitive man. Not only 'cause', we are to suppose, was within the range of his intellection, but 'something', 'principle of life', 'outward sign', 'mere animal life', 'spiritual as opposed to mere material', and heaven knows what else. Perverse; and yet for that very reason useful; for it pushes to a conclusion as logical as it is absurd, a view of mental history, which, still implicit in much that passes muster as anthropology, psychology, etc.—even as ordinary common sense—might easily prejudice an understanding of my meaning, if it were ignored without comment.

The truth is, of course, that Max Müller, like his predecessors, had only been able to look at 'meaning', and the history of meaning, from one imperfect point of view—that of abstraction. For in spite of frequent flights of imagination, the main road of his approach to language was the regulation one from philosophical logic or logical philosophy. Thus, he was an enthusiastic disciple of Kant—even to the Herculean extent of translating the *Critique of Pure Reason* into English. The full meanings of words are flashing, iridescent shapes like flames—ever-flickering vestiges of the slowly evolving consciousness beneath them. To the Locke-Müller-France way of thinking, on the contrary, they appear as solid chunks with definite boundaries and limits, to which other chunks may be added as occasion arises. Nevertheless, it is a mistake, and a mistake that is commonly made, to underrate Max Müller's semantic flights. The marvel is that with his materials and antecedents he was able to fly so high. Thus, even to this very question of metaphor he has an interesting contribution to make. We find him drawing a novel distinction between *radical* and *poetical* metaphors:

'I call it a radical metaphor when a root which means to shine is applied to form the names, not only of the fire or the sun, but of the spring of the year, the morning light, the brightness of thought, or the joyous outburst of hymns of praise. Ancient languages are brimful of such metaphors, and under the microscope of the etymologist almost every word discloses traces of its first metaphorical conception.

'From this we must distinguish *poetical* metaphor, namely, when a noun or verb, ready made and assigned to one definite object or action, is transferred poetically to another object or action. For instance, when the rays of the sun are called the hands or fingers of the sun.' *Science of Language*, p. 451.

In the next chapter I should like to discuss how far this distinction will carry us.

IV

MEANING AND MYTH

[1]

In his contrast between *radical* and *poetical* metaphor, Max Müller distinguished those 'figurative' expressions with which early languages abound from the similitudes deliberately invented by modern poets. This was an important step. Nevertheless, when we come to examine his definition of 'radical' metaphor and to inspect his examples, we can scarcely help being afflicted with grave misgivings. For we find that that definition is based on the old philologist's hypothesis of 'roots of speech'—the theory that every language started with a group of monosyllabic sounds, each of which expressed a simple, general notion. These general notions, it is supposed, were then applied to particular phenomena, among which they were subdivided by the addition of other words; and these latter words finally became the prefixes, suffixes, inflexions, etc., familiar to all students of the Aryan group of languages. Thus, to the root *hab* were added various little words implying the notion of particular number and person; but in course of time these coalesced, and the result was an inflected form such as the Latin *habuerunt*. Finally, by a process commonly alluded to as 'decay', these inflexions were lost and language returned once more to the use of separate words, as in the English *they have had*.

Now, from the grammatical point of view, it is hardly too much to say that this theory has been hopelessly discredited. Professor Jespersen, for example, in his *Progress in Language*, has put an overwhelmingly strong case for the opposite view, according to which the flexional (*hab-u-erunt*) form of language is the earlier, while the *isolating* or *root* (*they have had*) languages (of which Chinese is commonly taken as the most striking example) represent final—not first—stages of a long speech-evolution wherein English is already far advanced. 'The evolution of language'—so Professor Jespersen sums it up—'shows a progressive tendency from inseparable irregular conglomerations to freely and regularly combinable short elements.'

Again, if we approach the theory of roots from the *semantic* point of view, we shall find that here also it falls heavily to the ground. For it owes exactly the same defect as does that theory of metaphor and of a 'metaphorical period' which was elaborated in the last chapter. Moreover, the defect arises from the same cause, namely, that instead of starting from the present and working steadily backwards, the theorist insists on starting, as it were, from both ends at once. He has his idea, or prejudice, concerning the nature of primitive minds—an idea derived from sources quite outside his own study—and somehow or other he is determined to make his history of language coincide with that.

Consequently, just as, in considering metaphor, the

fact the he found language growing more and more figurative with every step into the past, did not prevent him from postulating an earliest period in which there were no 'figures' at all; so, the fact that he finds words growing longer and longer and meanings more and more individualized with every step into the past does not prevent him from depicting speech as *beginning* from monosyllables with *general* meanings ('roots'). Here it is necessary to point out that a meaning may be 'perceptual' (that is to say, the word's whole reference may be to some sensible object or process) and at the same time 'general' or 'abstract'. Anatole France's antithesis is, in fact, erroneous. It is just those meanings which attempt to be most exclusively material ('sensuel'), which are also the most generalized and abstract—i.e. remote from reality. Let us take the simple English word *cut.* Its reference is perfectly material; yet its meaning is at the same time more general and less particular, more abstract and less concrete, than some single word which should comprise in itself—let us say—all that we have to express to-day by the sentence: 'I cut this flesh with joy in order to sacrifice'. If it is impossible to cut a pound of flesh without spilling blood, it is even more impossible 'to cut'.[1]

Now it is an indisputable fact that, the further we look back into the history of the meanings of common words, the more closely we find them approximating to this latter, *concrete* type. Thus, even as recently as the date of the composition of the Fourth Gospel (John, ch. 3, v and viii) we can hear in the Greek πνεῦμα an echo of just

[1] See also Appendix II.

such an old, concrete, *undivided* meaning. This meaning (and therefore, in this case, practically the whole sense of the passage) is lost in the inevitably double English rendering of *spirit* (v) and *wind* (viii). There are any number of other examples. Here I shall be content to point to our seemingly arbitrary, and now purely verbal allotment of emotion to divers parts of the body, such as the *liver*, the *bowels*, the *heart*, where, in our own day, an old single meaning survives as two separate references of the same word—a physical and a psychic.[1]

According to Max Müller, it will be remembered, 'spiritus'—which is of course the Latin equivalent of πνεῦμα, acquired its apparently double meaning, because, at a certain early age, when it still meant simply *breath* or *wind*, it was deliberately employed *as a metaphor* to express 'the principle of life within man or animal'. All that can be replied to this is, that such an hypothesis is contrary to every indication presented by the study of the history of meaning; which assures us definitely that such a purely material content as 'wind', on the one hand, and on the other, such a purely abstract content as 'the principle of life within man or animal' are both *late* arrivals in human consciousness. Their abstractness and their simplicity are

[1] In *stomach* we may very possibly have an example of the transition stage — the actual moment of division. For in the twentieth century the expression 'I have no stomach to the business' is still by no means purely psychic in its content. It describes a very real physical sensation, or rather one which cannot be classified as either physical or psychic. Yet, on the analogy of the other words mentioned above, it is reasonable to suppose that, when a sufficient number of years has elapsed, the meaning of this word also may have been split by the evolution of our consciousness into two; and the physico-psychic experience in question will have become as incomprehensible to our posterity, as it is incomprehensible to most of us today that anyone should literally feel his 'bowels moved' by compassion.

alike evidence of long ages of intellectual evolution. So far from the psychic meaning of 'spiritus' having arisen because someone had the abstract idea, 'principle of life . . .' and wanted a word for it, the abstract idea 'principle of life' is itself a *product* of the old concrete *meaning* 'spiritus', which contained within itself the germs of both later significations. We must, therefore, imagine a time when 'spiritus' or πνεῦμα, or older words from which these had descended, meant neither *breath*, nor *wind*, nor *spirit*, nor yet all three of these things, but when they simply had *their own old peculiar meaning*, which has since, in the course of the evolution of consciousness, crystallized into the three meanings specified—and no doubt into others also, for which separate words had already been found by Greek and Roman times.

To sum up, if we assume, as it seems only reasonable to assume, that in the ages of speech preceding anything that can be touched by modern etymology the main stream of language, whose course is afterwards to become plainly visible to us, was already flowing in the *same* direction (i.e. from homogeneity towards dissociation and multiplicity) and not in an opposite one, what is the result? Both 'root' hypothesis and 'metaphor' hypothesis fall to the ground together. Müller's so-called *radical* metaphor, instead of being primitive, is seen to be one of the latest achievements of conscious linguistic development. A better name for it would be *synthetic* metaphor; and a better example, say, *gramophone*. 'Roots', far from being the germs of speech, are the product of ages of intellectual abstraction carried on, first, instinctively by ordinary speakers, and afterwards deliberately by the grammarians and philologists. The service rendered by these latter both to speech and to thought is of the utmost importance; their error merely lay in supposing that life actually created language after the manner in which their logic reconstructed it. They mistook elements for seeds—and called them roots.

[2]

Used with due caution, the mental progress of the individual from infancy to maturity is likely to provide some evidence of the mental history of the race; for the peculiar relation between phylogenesis and ontogenesis, which is summed up in the word 'recapitulation', quite evidently applies, within broad limits, to mind as well as body. Consequently, a consideration of the development of 'meaning' in the life-history of the individual would be pertinent to the matter in hand. There is clearly no room here to go into such a question in detail, but one may refer to the American psychologist, J. M. Baldwin,[1] who has pointed out how the adult observer constantly misreads his own logical processes into the child's mind. He shows how a child's apparent 'generalizations' are in reality single meanings, which it has not yet learnt to split up into two or more.[2] 'All psychic dualisms and

[1] See Appendix IV.

[2] For example, while every man is *papa*, this does not mean that the child uses the word *papa* to express a general idea, 'man'. He has no such general idea. He has one single meaning, 'papa', but it is a meaning which contains within itself the capacity to split up, or unfold or evolve into two separate ideas, 'Father' and 'man', of which one is more particular, and the other more general than the original 'portmanteau' meaning.

distinctions', he points out, 'are meanings in the sense that they are *differentiations from earlier and more simple* [*sic*] *apprehensions.*'

Finally, while it is a tiresome and stupid error to suppose that the childhood of races whose blood was afterwards to blossom into a Plato or a Shakespeare can be safely deduced from the present condition of peoples inhabiting Tasmania or the islands of the Pacific, nevertheless there are cases in which the one may conveniently be illustrated by the other. It is interesting, therefore, to find anthropologists telling us of the 'holophrase', or long, rambling conglomeration of sound and meaning, which is found among primitive and otherwise almost wordless peoples. Moreover, we hear again and again of primitive languages in which there are words for 'gum-tree', 'wattle-tree', etc., but none for 'tree'; and R. R. Marett, in his little book, *Anthropology*, remarks that in some crude tongues, although you can express twenty different kinds of cutting, you cannot say 'cut'. One could take many other examples from the chapter on *Language* in this book, to illustrate the distinction drawn above between concrete meanings and abstract meanings, a distinction which I have endeavoured to discuss a little more fully in an Appendix (IV).

[3]

We are now in a position to survey once more the apparent contradiction remarked above (III, 4–5) between aesthetic and philological judgements. On the one hand, the poet and the critic find language growing more and more poetic as they trace it back into the past. On the other, the Locke-Müller-France way of thinking sees the beginnings of language in a series of monosyllabic 'roots' with simple, perceptual references. What is the solution of this paradox? Hitherto, as far as I am aware, the only one worthy of the name has been that which is fairly common as vague idea, but which is found explicitly in Max Müller—that of the 'metaphorical period', a wonderful age when a race of anonymous and mighty poets took hold of a bald inventory and saturated it with poetic values. It is important to recollect that, as we saw in III, 4, these values are not merely poetic in the sense of causing pleasure, but also in the true, creative sense, as causing wisdom.

Recognition of this last fact should keep us from a certain tangle of loose thinking into which many evidently slip, to whom the existence of poetry is not an actual fact of phenomenal experience, nor its presence one of their measures of reality. For it is not infrequently suggested that the mere fact of direct connection with sensuous experience is enough to render language poetical. Thus, we find Macaulay[1] asserting that half-civilized nations are poetic *simply because* they perceive without abstracting, and absolutely regardless of *what* they perceive. And a similar view[2] is taken by Jespersen, who is otherwise content to dismiss the whole question of poetic values with the somewhat superficial reflection that after all 'we cannot all be poets'.[3] Maybe; but that very circum-

[1] *Essay on Milton*, p. 3. 'Nations, like individuals, first perceive and then abstract. They advance from particular images to general terms. Hence the vocabulary of an enlightened society is philosophical, that of a half-civilized people is poetical'. It is clear that Macaulay is here using the word 'perceive' in the ordinary, wider sense — the sense in which I use 'observe' (see II, 5, note).

[2] *Progress in Language*, § 273.

[3] *Ibid.*, § 79.

stance might surely have prompted him to investigate a little more closely the consequences of his own conclusion that once upon a time we all *were* poets!

Of these two theories, I have endeavoured to show my reasons for regarding the first as absurd and untenable. The second is, of course, not a solution at all. It merely shifts the locus of the problem; for we are still left asking *why* this direct perception should in itself have value as cause of wisdom. Indeed, the superficiality of such a view is so palpable that we can only suppose it to be the outcome of a consciousness to which the expression 'poetry as cause of wisdom' corresponds with no concrete experience, but is rather a contradiction in terms. There is, however, a third solution, and I suggest that it is one to which we are necessarily led by all that has gone before. It is this: that these poetic, and *apparently* 'metaphorical' values were latent in meaning from the beginning. In other words, you may imply, if you choose, with Dr. Blair, that the earliest words in use were 'the names of sensible, material objects' *and nothing more*—only, in that case, you must suppose the 'sensible objects' themselves to have been something more; you must suppose that they were not, as they appear to be at present, isolated, or detached, from thinking and feeling.[1] Afterwards, in the development of language and thought, these single meanings split up into contrasted pairs—the abstract and the concrete, particular and general, objective and subjective. And the poesy felt by us to reside in ancient language consists just in this, that, out of our later, analytic, 'subjective' consciousness, a consciousness which has been brought about

[1] See also Appendix IV.

along with, and partly because of, this splitting up of meaning, we are led back to experience the original unity.

Thus, the sunstruck or 'meaningless' man, into whose consciousness we endeavoured to enter in II, 5, is in no sense whatever (as Anatole France, for instance, assumed) an analagon of primitive man. To make him that, we should have to conceive of him—so far from being meaningless—as literally resounding with all manner of meaning, and moreover, with meaning such that, if he could but communicate it to us, we should be listening to poetry.

Then what is a true metaphor? In the same essay of Shelley's, from which I have already quoted, he cites a fine passage from Bacon's *Advancement of Learning*:

'Neither are these only similitudes, as men of narrow observation may conceive them to be, but the same footsteps of nature, treading or printing upon several subjects or matters.'[1]

This is the answer. It is these 'footsteps of nature' whose noise we hear alike in primitive language and in the finest metaphors of poets. Men do not *invent* those mysterious relations between separate external objects, and between objects and feelings or ideas, which it is the function of poetry to reveal. These relations exist independently, not indeed of Thought, but of any individual thinker. And according to whether the footsteps are echoed in primitive language or, later on, in the made metaphors of poets, we hear them after a different fashion and for different reasons. The language of primitive men reports them as direct perceptual experience. The speaker has observed a unity, and is not therefore himself conscious of *relation*. But we, in the

[1] *Advancement of Learning*, II v. 3.

development of consciousness, have lost the power to see this one as one. Our sophistication, like Odin's, has cost us an eye; and now it is the language of poets, in so far as they create true metaphors, which must *restore* this unity conceptually, after it has been lost from perception. Thus, the 'before-unapprehended' relationships of which Shelley spoke, are in a sense 'forgotten' relationships. For though they were never yet apprehended, they were at one time seen. And imagination can see them again.

In the whole development of consciousness, therefore, we can trace the operation of two opposing principles, or forces. Firstly, there is the force by which, as we saw, single meanings tend to split up into a number of separate and often isolated concepts. This is the τὸ λογίζειν[1] of Shelley's *Essay*. We can, if we choose, characterize it as non-poetic—even as anti-poetic, so long as we remember that for the *appreciation* of language as poetry, this principle is every whit as necessary as the other. The second principle is one which we find given us, to start with, as the nature of language itself at its birth. It is the principle of living unity. Considered subjectively, it observes the resemblances between things, whereas the first principle marks the differences,[2] is interested in knowing what things *are*,

[1] *A Defence of Poetry*, p. 1. I keep his term, though Liddell and Scott give λογίζεσθαι only.

[2] Cf. Bacon; *Novum Organum*, i. 55.

Maximum et velut radicale discrimen ingeniorum, quoad philosophiam et scientias, illud est: quod alia ingenia sint fortiora et aptiora ad notandas rerum differentias: alia, ad notandas rerum similitudines. Ingenia enim constantia et acuta figere contemplationes, et morari, et haerere in omne subtilitate differentiarum possunt; ingenia autem sublimia et discursiva etiam tenuissimas et catholicas rerum similitudines et agnoscunt at componunt: utrumque autem ingenium facile labitur in excessum, prensando aut gradus rerum, aut umbras.

whereas the first discerns what they are not. Accordingly, at a later stage in the evolution of consciousness, we find it operative in individual poets, enabling them (τὸ ποιεῖν) to intuit relationships which their fellows have forgotten—relationships which they must *now* express as metaphor. Reality, once self-evident, and therefore not conceptually experienced, but which can *now* only be reached by an effort of the individual mind—this is what is contained in a true poetic metaphor; and every metaphor is 'true'[1] only in so far as it contains such a reality, or hints at it. The world, like Dionysus, is torn to pieces by pure intellect; but the poet is Zeus; he has swallowed the heart of the world; and he can reproduce it as a living body.

It is really not at all surprising that philologists should have had such a vivid hallucination of metaphor bending over the cradle of meaning. For the distinction is a distinction of agent rather than of function, and the principle is indeed one. Nevertheless it is better to keep the definition of the label *metaphor* within bounds and thus to deny it to these early meanings, which appear in the world without individualized poetic effort. *Figure* and *figurative*, on the other hand—as long as we disentangle them carefully in our minds from the modern expression 'figure of speech', may justly be applied, owing to the perceptual or aesthetic, the *pictorial*, form in which these unitary meanings first manifest in consciousness. Not an empty 'root meaning to shine', but the same definite spiritual reality which was beheld on the one hand in what has since become pure human thinking; and on the other hand, in what has since become physical light; not an

[1] See also Appendix III.

abstract conception, but the echoing footsteps of the goddess Natura—not a metaphor but a living Figure.

[4]

Perhaps nothing could be more damning to the 'root' conception of language than the ubiquitous phenomenon of the Myth. Now myth, at any rate for the Aryan peoples, is intimately bound up with the early history of meaning. It is the same with innumerable words; if one traces them back far enough, one reaches a period at which their meanings had a mythical content. To take such English words as *panic, hero, fortune, fury, earth, North, South*, is merely to lay hands on the most obvious examples. A glance at the *Vedas* will make much clearer the enormously wide scope of this historical phenomenon. Yet the 'root' theory of language and its affiliated conceptions either have nothing to say on this head, or they suggest the most sterile trivialities. The reason of this is fairly plain. Upon such a view the myths must be the product of that same mysterious 'metaphorical period' when the inventive ingenuity of humanity is said to have burgeoned and sprouted as never before or since. Thus Max Müller, who perceived very clearly the intimate bond connecting myth with metaphor and meaning, was actually obliged to characterize the myth as a kind of *disease* of language.[1] Such a point of view is barely worth discussing, or rather, to the genuine critic, it is *not* worth discussing. For, for him, the poetic wisdom-values which he finds over and over again in myth would themselves be an immediate and sufficient answer. The word 'disease' is meaningless in such a connection.

[1] *The Science of Language*, II, 454 ff.

On the other hand, the more widely accepted 'naturalistic' theory of myths is very little more satisfactory. For it is obliged to lean just as heavily on the same wonderful metaphorical period. The only difference is this, that for an extinct race of mighty poets it substitutes an extinct race of mighty philosophers. In either case, we must admit that the posthumous obscurity of these intellectual giants is ill-deserved, considering that the world owes to them (to take only one example) practically the entire contents of Lemprière's *Classical Dictionary*. The remoter ancestors of Homer, we are given to understand, observing that it was darker in winter than in summer, immediately decided that there must be some 'cause' for this 'phenomenon', and had no difficulty in tossing off the 'theory' of, say, Demeter and Persephone, to account for it. A good name for this kind of banality—the fruit, as it is, of *projecting post-logical thoughts back into a pre-logical age*—would perhaps be 'Logomorphism'. Whatever we call it, there is no denying that it is at present extraordinarily widespread, being indeed taken for granted in all the most reputable circles. Imagination, history, bare common sense—these, it seems, are as nothing beside the paramount necessity that the great Mumbo Jumbo, the patent, double-million magnifying Inductive Method, should be allowed to continue contemplating its own ideal reflection—a golden age in which every man was his own Newton, in a world dropping with apples. Only when poesy, who is herself alive, looks backward, does she see at a glance how much younger is the Tree of Knowledge than the Tree of Life.[1]

[1] See also Appendix IV.

[5]

For to the poetic understanding myth presents an altogether different face. These fables are like corpses which, fortunately for us, remain visible after their living content has departed out of them. In the *Classical Dictionary*, the student of poetic diction finds delicately mummified for his inspection any number of just those old single meanings, which the differentiating, analytic process already referred to has desiccated and dissected. Goethe gave symbolical expression to this striking fact at the end of Act III, Part II, of his *Faust*. Here, however, a single example must suffice. We find poet after poet expressing in metaphor and simile the analogy between death and sleep and winter, and again between birth and waking and summer, and these, once more, are constantly made the types of a spiritual experience—of the death in the individual soul of its accidental part and the putting on of incorruption. 'Except a corn of wheat fall into the ground, and die, it abideth alone; but if it die, it bringeth forth much fruit.'

Now by our definition of a 'true metaphor', there should be some older, undivided 'meaning' from which all these logically disconnected, but poetically connected ideas have sprung. And in the beautiful myth of Demeter and Persephone we find precisely such a meaning. In the myth of Demeter the ideas of waking and sleeping, of summer and winter, of life and death, of mortality and immortality are all lost in one pervasive meaning. This is why so many theories are brought forward to account for the myths. The naturalist is right when he connects the myth with the phenomena of nature, but wrong if he deduces it solely from these. The psycho-analyst is right when he connects the myth with 'inner' (as we now call them) experiences, but wrong if he deduces it solely from these. Mythology is the ghost of concrete meaning. Connections between discrete phenomena, connections which are now apprehended as metaphor, were once perceived as immediate realities. As such the poet strives, by his own efforts, to see them, and to make others see them, again.

In a work with the present title, one need have no hesitation in making such round assertions; for either they are true, or poetry itself is a dream and a disease. 'It is easily seen', wrote Emerson, referring especially to the kind of metaphor or analogy which relates the 'inner' experience to the 'outer':

'that there is nothing lucky or capricious in these analogies, but that they are constant, and pervade nature. These are not the dreams of a few poets, here and there, but man is an analogist, and studies relations in all objects. He is placed in the centre of beings, and a ray of relation passes from every other being to him. And neither can man be understood without these objects, nor these objects without man. All the facts in natural history taken by themselves have no value, but are barren like a single sex. But marry it to human history, and it is full of life. . . .

'Because of this radical correspondence between visible things and human thoughts, savages, who have only what is necessary, converse in figures. As we go back in history, language becomes more picturesque, until its infancy, when it is all poetry; or all spiritual facts are represented by natural symbols.'[1]

[1] Emerson; *Nature*, Ch. IV on 'Language'.

V

LANGUAGE AND POETRY

[1]

Thus, a history of language written, not from the logician's, but from the poet's point of view, would proceed somewhat in the following manner: it would see in the concrete vocabulary which has left us the mythologies the world's first 'poetic diction'. Moving forward, it would come, after a long interval, to the earliest ages of which we have any written record—the time of the *Vedas* in India, the time of the *Iliad* and *Odyssey* in Greece. And at this stage it would find meaning still suffused with myth, and Nature all alive in the thinking of man.

The gods are never far below the surface of Homer's language—hence its unearthly sublimity. They are the springs of action and stand in place of what we think of as personal qualities. Agamemnon is warned of Zeus in a dream, Telemachus, instead of 'plucking up courage', meets the goddess Athene and walks with her into the midst of the hostile suitors, and the whole earth buds into blossom, as Zeus is mingled with Hera on the nuptial couch.

Millions of spiritual beings walk the earth. . . . And these august beings, speaking now from the mouths of the characters, and again passing and repassing invisible among them, dissolve into a sort of *largior aether*, which the Homeric heroes breathe all day; so that we, too, breathe it in the language they speak—in their ῥοδοδάκτυλος ἠώς, their ἱερὸν ἦμαρ, in the sinewy strength of those thundering epithets which, for all their conventionality, never fail to impart life and warmth to the lines.

Meanwhile, the historian would note how the anti-poetic, or purely rational, had begun to take effect. He would find meanings splitting up in the manner previously described and language beginning to change its character, to lose its intrinsic life. He might note, also, that the increased action of this principle was accompanied by the birth of hitherto unknown antitheses, such as those between truth and myth, between prose and poetry, and again between an objective and a subjective world; so that now, for the first time, it becomes possible to distinguish the *content* of a word from its *reference*.

He might then, perhaps, look to the history of philosophy for some indication of the moment at which the ascending rational principle and the descending poetic principle (for, in certain respects, we can think of them as of two buckets in a well) are passing one another. If so, I think he would fix on the prominence in men's minds of the metaphysical problem of 'universals'. For when the number of general ideas arrived at by abstraction (see IV, I) is rapidly increasing, and yet there is still a strong sense of the old, concrete, unitary meanings, it is natural that the co-existence of two kinds of universal should arouse confusion. Are universals real beings, it is asked, or mere classifying abstractions in the minds of men, evolved for the convenience of quick thinking? The latter (Nominalist-Conceptualist) verdict, if applied indiscriminately to *all* universals, may be compared with the error, noted in IV, 2, by which an adult thinker reads his own generalizations into a child's mind.

Thus the old, instinctive consciousness of single meanings, which comes down to us as the Greek myths, is already fighting for its life by Plato's time as the doctrine of Platonic Ideas (not 'abstract', though this word is often erroneously used in English translations); Aristotle's logic and his Categories, *as interpreted by his followers*, then tend to concentrate attention exclusively on the *abstract* universals, and so to destroy the balance; and then again the forms and entelechies of Aristotle are brought to life in the poetry of Dante as the Heavenly Hierarchies; and, yet again, Nominalism, with its legacy of modern empirical philosophy and science, obscures men's vision of all but the abstract universals.[1]

Thus would he find the general progress obscured and varied by all sorts of particular forces operating in the history of civilization. For example, if he chose the Aryan community of speakers as his canvas, he would have to

[1] Naturally, this sketchy account must be met half-way, and with considerable delicacy of apprehension, if it is to have any truth and meaning. Any rigidly regular development of the two principles is out of the question. Innate differences between mind and mind, together with the increasing intercommunication of recorded thought and its transmission from past to present, are always at work to spread the process. The two principles themselves, however, and their historical development, are none the less realities because, like the aesthetic values, they do not force themselves on the attention of the percipient, but await the exertion of his own imaginative activity.

consider, on the one hand, the history of Aryan language and Aryan consciousness as a whole, and, on the other, the rise and decay—within that single entity—of the various national languages and national spirits among which it has been distributed. Each of these, he would probably find, repeats in its own compass, and in varying degrees, the broad lines of evolution of the whole. Within certain limits, we should be brought to see that, in poetic character, the Latin language is to the Greek as the later stages of Greek are to its own earlier stages; and, also, as the later stages of English are to its earlier stages.

[2]

For example, there is a certain half-spurious element in the appreciation of poetry, with which everyone will be familiar, when one takes delight, not only in what is said and in the way it is said, but in a sense of difficulties overcome—of an obstreperous medium having been masterfully subdued. It is a kind of architectural pleasure. One feels that the poet is working in solid masses, not in something fluid. One is reminded by one's very admiration that 'words are stubborn things'. In English literature Milton's verse presents a particularly striking example of what I mean; and I select a quotation almost at random, hoping that it will make my meaning clear:

Fall'n Cherube, to be weak is miserable
Doing or Suffering: but of this be sure,
To do ought good never will be our task,
But ever to do ill our sole delight,

As being the contrary to his high will
Whom we resist. If then his Providence
Out of our evil seek to bring forth good,
Our labour must be to pervert that end,
And out of good still to find means of evil.

It is demonstrable that this architectural element in poetic diction is something which only arises at a certain stage in the development of a language. It is there in the iambics of the Attic dramatists, but not in Homer's hexameters; yet it is not entirely foreign to the spirit of the hexameter, for it is conspicuous in Virgil:

At regina dolos (quis fallere possit amantem?)
Praesensit motusque excepit prima futuros,
Omnia tuta timens. Eadem impia Fama furenti
Detulit armari classem cursumque parari.

Indeed Virgil's poetry is an excellent example. It is in his most famous and most often-quoted passages that we find that exquisite hint, as it were, of the jig-saw puzzle; and, along with it, that exact use of quantitative values and the marvellous interweaving of these with the different stresses which would normally be given to the sentences, in accordance with their emotional content.

This subtle music is the very life of the *Æneid*. But it is a life that is imparted by Virgil himself, in his arrangement of the words, rather than one inherent in the Latin language. There is quite another kind of life in the *Iliad*—that of the old Greek language itself. Compare the vigour and brilliance of Homer's epithets with the best equivalents that Virgil could find for them: *celer* for πτερόεις, *curvæ naves* for νῆες ἀμφιελίσσαι, *flumine pulchro* for καλλιρρόῳ ποτάμῳ, etc. And we find the same contrast—a contrast, as it were between movement and rest—working itself out in broader curves in the descriptions of the shields (*Iliad*, xviii and *Æneid*, viii, 607–731), where Homer instinctively translates the description of motionless objects into action, while Virgil finds it natural to employ the static mode of 'here is . . .', 'there is . . .'.[1]

There is a strong tendency in the Greek language, with its reckless profusion of double epithets, its looser word-order, and its nervous, restless twitchings of grammatical particles, to make itself felt as a living, muscular organism rather than as a structure; and it is quite in harmony with this that the terminology of grammar, most of which is derived from Greek, should have originated in so many cases as physical or physiological metaphor.[1] In Horace's Sapphics and Alcaics, on the other hand, the architectural element practically reaches its zenith. And again, if we turn to the history of English, I do not think we can say that we find this architectural element at all pronounced until the seventeenth century. It strikes us, for instance, in Milton and in the Metaphysicals, and frequently afterwards, but hardly in Chaucer or Shakespeare.

To characterize further the difference between what I have ventured to describe as the *fluid* type of poetry and the later, *architectural* type: in the later, elisions tend to become less frequent, whilst (in verse) the number of syllables in a single foot or time-interval grows less easily variable.

[1] Moreover, Homer shows us Hephaestus *actually fashioning* the shield, whereas Virgil speaks as a spectator examining the finished product.

[2] E.g. πτῶσις, ἄρθρον, συνδέσμος, etc.

Another test is this: it is much harder to convey the *full* effect of poetry of the architectural type with the *voice*. The eye seems to be necessary as well, so that the shape of a whole line or period can be taken in instantaneously. The actual sounds have grown more fixed and rigid and monotonous; the stresses accordingly are more subtle, depending upon the way in which the emotional meaning —as it were—struggles against this rigidity; and this produces a music different indeed, but none the less lovely because it is often audible only to the inward ear. The fluid type of verse, on the other hand, is made for reciting or singing aloud and probably gains more than it loses by this method of delivery.

[3]

It is especially interesting that we find this transition of poetry from an organic to a relatively structural character reflected in the formal history of language itself. For assuming that Jespersen's view of the direction of progress is correct, we can trace the change from a flexional state, in which word-*order* is relatively unfixed and unimportant, towards a final state in which word-order is fixed and so essential to the expression of meaning that a slight change may actually reverse the sense—as in the English sentence 'The Gentlemen beat the Players'. Of known languages, Chinese is again, apparently, the furthest developed in this direction. To the poet or critic, a language which has reached this last stage presents the appearance of a kind of crystallization, the semantic elements requiring to be rearranged in a series of kaleidoscopic jerks. Whereas in a language still at the 'flexional' stage the meaning, vaguer in its outlines, but more muscular and alive, can afford to leave even the words themselves as though still in motion. The reader has not the same sense of their being set and fixed in their places.[1]

Here it is worth remarking on a phenomenon in the history of philology which comes in for some ridicule at the hands of Jespersen. I mean the pronounced tendency to refer to the flexional type of language as 'strong' and the analytic type as 'weak'. In the same way the loss of inflexions has long been regarded in philological circles as a symptom of 'decay' or 'senility'. Jespersen attributes the origin of this incorrigible philological prejudice to pedantic preoccupation with Latin and Greek; its maintenance he assigns to blind tradition. He sums up in a masterly manner the enormous advantages in point of economy and lucidity which the analytic language possesses over its flexional ancestor and pronounces himself unable to see any meaning in the use of such a word as 'senility' in such a connection.

In my view, however, this well-worn terminology of the philologists springs from a kind of true instinct for poetic values. Mr. Jespersen, in his *Progress in Language*, builds argument upon argument to prove that the historical development of language is indeed 'progressive' and not a kind of falling away from grace, as his predecessors held. These arguments are absolutely convincing and require no comment, as long as we remember that, to the author, 'progress' in the history of consciousness does not merely include, but is synonymous with an increasing ability to

[1] For a change of meaning of this nature see VII, 2 and 3.

think abstract thoughts. This fact grows more and more apparent as one reads on, until at last one realizes that, where Coleridge failed, Mr. Jespersen has succeeded in 'taming down his mind to think poetry a sport or an occupation for idle hours'. But I have already referred to the summary manner in which the distinguished Danish philologist dismisses this side of his subject.

The poetic historian of language, therefore, would certainly have to consider such a question as the following: is there some period in the development of a language at which, all other factors being excluded, it is fittest to become the vehicle of great poetry; and is this followed by a kind of decline? We might suppose that at a certain stage the rational, abstracting, formal principle will have stayed and confined the primal flow of meaning to an extent which is just exquisite; that this is the moment of all moments for the great poet to step in; and that in a century or so the balance will have been destroyed, the formal principle have run ahead, so that in the greatest poetry we shall have henceforth that Miltonic flavour—delightful indeed, but perhaps a thought less divine—of cyclopean achievement and rest after labour. It can hardly be doubted that this period would be found to bear *some* recognizable relation to that point of balance between the rational and the poetic, to which I referred earlier in the chapter. But I may not put all this forward as more than a suggestion; for the poetic history of language which I have attempted to sketch upon air would need for its actual bringing down to earth a far wider culture and an acquaintance with a great many more languages and literatures than I can lay claim to. *Faciant meliora potentes.*

VI

THE POET

[1]

In II, 3, and again in III, 5, the question was raised of the responsibility of individuals for poetic values. Now an answer to this question is really implicit in what has since been said. It will no doubt be realized therefore that the extent of this responsibility is variable, *increasing* with the 'progress' of language in any community of speakers. For it has been shown that poetic values abound, as *meaning*, in the early stages of those languages with which we are familiar; this meaning has then been traced back to its source in the theocratic, 'myth-thinking' period, and it has been shown that the myths, which represent the earliest meanings, were not the arbitrary creations of 'poets', but the natural expression of man's being and consciousness at the time. These primary 'meanings' were *given*, as it were, by Nature, but the very condition of their being given was that they could not at the same time be apprehended in full consciousness; they could not be *known*, but only experienced, or lived. At this time, therefore, individuals cannot be said to have been responsible for the production of poetic values. Not man was creating, but the gods—or, in psychological jargon, his 'unconscious'. But with the development of consciousness, as this 'given' poetic meaning decreases more and more, the individual poet gradually steps into his own. In place of the simple, given *meaning*, we find the *metaphor*—a real creation of the individual—though, in so far as it is true, it is only re-creating, registering as *thought*, one of those eternal facts which may already have been experienced in perception.

We have seen also how this change in the nature of poetry is intimately connected with the development of the rational principle (by which meaning is split up) at the expense of the poetic principle. Owing to familiar associations, this use of the word 'poetic' may still be misleading, unless we are willing to consider it a little further. In II, 3, it was pointed out as matter of immediate experience that what is poetry to the reader or hearer need not have been poetry to its maker. This may now be put more strongly: inasmuch as man is *living* the poetry of which he is the maker, and as long as he is so doing, it *cannot* be poetry to him. In order to *appreciate* it, he himself must also exist, consciously, outside it; for otherwise the 'felt change of consciousness' cannot come about. Now nothing but the rational, or logistic, principle can endow him with this subjective—*self*—consciousness.[1] Hence it was justly inferred (IV, 3) that the functioning of the rational principle is indispensable, if *appreciation* is to take place. The absolute rational principle is that which makes conscious of poetry but cannot create it; the absolute poetic principle is that which creates poetry but cannot make conscious of it. It

[1] For a fuller treatment of this, see Appendix IV.

follows from this that, the further back we look, and the more we see what I have called the poetic principle active in language, the less appreciation of poetry shall we find. And though this may at first sight look startling, I believe there is no doubt that it is true. Let us, however, consider a few opinions on the subject.

Macaulay, it is true, regards the fact that (according to Plato) the old Rhapsodists could scarcely recite Homer without falling into convulsions as evidence of a greater capacity in the ancients for 'enjoying poetry'! In later ages, he says, 'Men will talk about the old poets, and comment on them, and to a certain degree enjoy them. But they will scarcely be able to conceive the effect which poetry produced on their ruder ancestors, the agony, the ecstasy, the plenitude of belief. . . . The Mohawk hardly feels the scalping-knife while he shouts his death-song.'

And Gibbon takes a similar line in his characteristic account of the Teutonic bards:

'Among a polished people, a taste for poetry is rather an amusement of the fancy, than a passion of the soul. And yet, when in calm retirement we peruse the combats described by Homer or Tasso, we are insensibly seduced by the fiction and feel a momentary glow of martial ardour. But how faint, how cold is the sensation which a peaceful mind can receive from solitary study! It was in the hour of battle, or in the feast of victory, that the bards celebrated the glory of heroes of ancient days, the ancestors of those warlike chieftains who listened with transport to their artless but animated strains. The view of arms and of danger heightened the effect of the military song; and the passions which it tended to excite, the desire of fame, and the contempt of death, were the habitual sentiments of a German mind.'

Now if we examine these modest admissions of aesthetic inferiority a little farther, we shall find them to be based on the following assumption: that human experience must have been 'faint', unless it produce some violent physical effect. This childish materialism scarcely needs refuting. We may, however, use the indiscretion of two famous historians as a reminder that any attempt to unseal the sources of poetry is certain to be abortive, unless the critic can distinguish between the mood of creation and the mood of appreciation—a distinction which the piercing gaze of Shelley had, as usual, no difficulty in remarking:

'In the infancy of the world, neither poets themselves nor their auditors are fully aware of the excellence of poetry: for it acts in a divine and unapprehended manner, beyond and above consciousness; and it is reserved for future generations to contemplate and measure the mighty cause and effect in all the strength and splendour of their union.' *A Defence of Poetry.*

Thus, it must be understood that when I speak of the poetic I mean what many people would prefer to call the 'creative'. The poet is a man speaking to men. In order that 'poetry', strictly so called, should exist, an appreciating imagination, in which aesthetic experience can light up, is of course as necessary as the creative activity of the poet. And so, although the poetic *principle* in language has waned since Homer's day, poetry as inner experience has increased. The light of conscious poesy which can irradiate a modern imagination, as it comes into contact with, say, the Homeric hexameters, is not to be compared with such fitful aesthetic gleams as must indeed have flared up now and again amid the host of grosser pleasures preoccupying the dim self-consciousness of his own (probably half-intoxicated) audience.

[2]

Precisely parallel to the history of civilization in this respect, is the aesthetic history of the individual. One need only refer to Wordsworth's theory and practice alike for a full statement of the way in which the child's experiences can acquire poetic value *as remembered* by the conscious, full-grown man. The old, single, living meanings (IV, 2) which the individual, like the race, splits up and so kills, as he grows, are allowed to impinge *as memory* on the adult consciousness; and the result is pure aesthetic experience. This is the true sense in which the child is father of the man.

Thus, in both cases, the individual is thrown more and more upon his own resources as time goes on: he can draw upon his own and his race's childhood for wisdom, and the gaining of that wisdom will be accompanied by aesthetic experience. The amount of knowledge which is thus accessible, however, will obviously be limited. Whatever vast truths may have been laid open to the vague, yet living, consciousness of his ancestors or his infancy, it is certain that history and memory will actually have *preserved* no more than a fragment. In this respect our human consciousness is something like a man who should try, by turning round, to see the back of his head in a mirror. For the impulses to record and to remember can only come into it along with the very change that begins to obscure perception of what is most worth remembering. If the later man wishes to increase this limited store of wisdom, therefore, he has to look for some way of renewing the immediate activity of the poetic principle. No longer does he find this operative of its own accord in the meanings of words; indeed, the modern poet is in some sense, as we saw in the last chapter, in the position of having to fight *against* words, whereas the primitive bard was carried forward on their meanings like Arion on the dolphin's back. Where then does the modern poet find again this poetic principle that is dying out of language? Where? Nowhere but in himself. The same creative activity, once operative in meaning without man's knowledge or control, and only recognized long afterwards, when he awoke to contemplate, as it were, what he had written in his sleep, this is now to be found within his own consciousness. And it calls him to become the true creator, the maker of meaning itself.

[3]

I have said 'within his own consciousness', but this expression, too, is misleading unless it is understood historically. The poet, purely as creator, cannot even today be regarded as a self-conscious individual, for such consciousness is impossible without rational analytic thought. In so far as his own poetic activity comes within his knowledge and control, in so far as he can *appreciate*, and so correct, his own poetry, or choose what he will write, he is not maker, but comparer, or judge; and he cannot be both simultaneously. There is a mood of creation and a mood of appreciation. This was no doubt at the back of the critic's mind who said that 'to write well of love a man must be in love, but to correct his writing he must be out of it again'.

Yet if the intellectual and active powers are, in Emerson's phrase, 'exclusive', the interval of time which must elapse between their alternations need not be fixed. Nor is it. We may realize the delicacy and rapidity with which they must be considered as interacting, if we reflect that *the bare fact of verbal expression* implies the operation of the rational principle. Outside proper names, every word in every language is a generalization, and, when we speak of the poetic values being 'given' in early language, we must not lose sight of the fact that these values were already fading, were already but relics of still more living values which must have obtained in consciousness before the birth of speech. Without reason—and reason in the rationalist's, not the Coleridgian sense—there could have been no speech, as we understand it, at all. It follows that the poet's power of *expression* will be dependent on the development of the rational principle in himself.[1] It is from the Gorgon's head, petrifying life into the stone of abstraction, that Pegasus is born. A great poet, too, spells a great intellect, and such an one is fairly sure to have the faculty of delighting in abstract thought. Is it necessary to cite the acute analytical thinking in Keats's and Shelley's letters, the flawless forensic armour of Milton's Satan, the discursive vigour of the *Paradiso*, or the logical fisticuffs of Shakespeare's comic characters?

[1] Cf. Aristotle (*De Anima*, III, 2, v.), *ἡ γὰρ τοῦ ποιητικοῦ καὶ κινητικοῦ ἐνεργεία ἐν τῷ πάσχοντι ἐγγίγνεται.* I would rather not attempt to translate this into English.

But apart from the more subtle interaction of the two principles which is implied in the mere existence of language, we have to consider the time-interval between the mood of poetic creation proper and the mood of appreciation, or of mere inactivity, if we wish to grasp the reality behind the expression 'within his own consciousness', which I employed above.

Now when we look back at the attitude which his fellow men have maintained towards the poet, from the time when they first became conscious of him as something apart from themselves, we shall again, I think, find something in the nature of a 'progress'. First, the poet was conceived of as being definitely 'possessed' by some foreign being, a god or angel, who gave utterance through his mouth, and gave it only as and when it chose. Then the divine power was said to be 'breathed in' to the poet, by beings such as the Muses, at special times and places, over which he had some measure of control, in that he could go himself to the places and 'invoke' the Muse. Finally this 'breathing in' or *inspiration* took on the more metaphorical sense which it has today—defintely retaining, however, the original suggestion of a diminished *self*-consciousness. Inspiration! It was the only means, we used to be told, by which poetry could be written, and the poet himself hardly knew what it was—a kind of divine wind, perhaps, which blew where it listed and might fill his sails at some odd moment after he had whistled for it all day in vain. So we were told not long ago; but today we are more inclined to think of inspiration as a mood—a mood that may come and go in the course of a morning's work.

Thus, throughout the history of poetry we can discern,

reflected at any rate in opinion, a gradual reduction of the inevitable interval between the two moods, which remain nevertheless incompatible in their essential nature; till to-day this huge change from poetic to appreciative, from creative to contemplative, which the material he is working in—language—has itself been performing in one direction over a period measured by millenniums, flickers with dazzling rapidity in the being of a single poet. Not only from one day or hour to another is there alternation of mood: his whole consciousness oscillates while his pen is poised in the air, and he deliberates an epithet.

This, then, is as much as is meant by saying that the poet now finds the material of his metaphorical creation 'in his own consciousness'. And if the two moods must for ever remain incompatible, there is nothing to prevent us looking forward to a time—to be brought in, let us say, by that excellent labour-saving device known to the nineteenth century as 'evolution', or even, *faute de mieux*, by the personal endeavour of poets themselves towards increased self-knowledge and self-control—when, to use a mathematical expression, the frequency of these oscillations may have increased to infinity; at which point at last the poet shall be creating out of full self-consciousness.

VII

THE MAKING OF MEANING (I)

[1]

It is, then, impossible—on an absolutely unprejudiced interpretation of experience—not to recognize two different sorts of poetry, the later of which, having arisen out of the former by imperceptible gradation, exists side by side with it and eventually tends to replace it. 'The poetry', says Hegel, 'of ages in which the prosaic spirit is already developed is essentially distinct from that of primitive epochs, among peoples whose imagination is still wholly poetic.'[1]

We have, however, already seen that that earlier kind of poetry—the instinctive kind, if we choose to call it so—lives on to some extent in the meanings of words, even after the other has begun to replace it; so that in any particular poem it is still a question of disentangling the two elements (cf. II, 3). And when we have done so, we shall find that, in the later kind of poetry, for which the indivi-

[1] *Philosophy of Fine Art.* Oswald Spengler, in *The Decline of the West,* has a great deal to say on the whole nature and meaning of this 'prosaic spirit', tracing its increasing expression in nearly every walk of life, in the historical development both of our own civilization and of the the great civilizations of the past.

dual poet is increasingly responsible—in which, as we saw, he has in certain respects to fight *against* language, making up the poetic deficit out of his private balance—in this kind it is perfectly true to call the poet the creator, or re-creator of meaning itself. For, if re-creation is strictly the more accurate term, yet creation, besides being established in current aesthetic terminology, is more truly fitted to the majesty of the idea. Surely no critic with enough metaphysical wit to be interested in the question at all would deny that 'creation', as an aesthetic term, signifies, not some fantastic 'creation out of nothing', but the bringing farther into consciousness of something which already exists as unconscious life? It is no disservice, then, to this frightfully abused word to emphasize its real connotation.

Now, apart from the actual invention of new words (an art in which many poets have excelled), the principal means by which this creation of meaning is achieved is—as has already been pointed out—metaphor. But it must be remembered that *any* specifically *new* use of a word or phrase is really a metaphor, since it attempts to arouse cognition of the unknown by suggestion from the known. I will take an example: the painter's expression *point of view* was a metaphor the first time it was used (probably by Coleridge) with a psychological content. This content is today one of its accepted meanings—indeed, it is the most familiar one—but it could only have become so *after* passing, explicitly or implicitly, through the earlier stage of metaphor. In other words, either Coleridge or somebody else either said or thought (I am of course putting it a little crudely) '*x* is to the mind what *point of view* is to an observer of landscape'. And in so doing he enriched the content of the expression 'point of view' just as Shakespeare enriched the content of 'balm' (and of 'sleep', too) when he called sleep the 'balm of hurt minds' ('sleep is to hurt minds what balm is to hurt bodies'). Reflection will show that the 'new' use of an epithet—that is to say, its application to a substantive with which it has not hitherto been coupled—is also a concealed metaphor.[1]

In the present chapter I shall attempt to trace a single, predominantly 'literary' example of the continuous creation of meaning in the above sense.

[2]

English schoolboys are generally taught to translate the Latin verb 'ruo' by one of two words, *rush* or *fall*. And it does indeed 'mean' both these things; but, because it means both and because it also means a great deal more, neither rendering alone is really an adequate equivalent. In the classical contexts themselves it nearly always carries with it a larger sense of swift, disastrous movement—'ruit arduus aether' of a deluge of rain, and again, 'Fiat Justitia,

[1] Thus, when Blake wrote:

> *Then I made a rural pen*
> *And I stained the water clear . . .*

his semantic act can be seen, in retrospect, to have contained *implicitly* the judgement: 'These hitherto unapprehended attributes are to my pen what the attributes connoted by the epithet *rural* are to the objects to which that epithet is customarily applied'.

But to say that it contained this judgement implicitly is not to say that it was equivalent to this judgement. On the contrary; for logical judgements, by their nature, can only *render more explicit* some one part of a truth *already implicit in their terms*. But the poet makes the terms themselves. He does not make judgements, therefore; he only makes them possible—and only he makes them possible.

ruat coelum'. Why is this? The Greek ῥέω, 'to flow', and similar words in other European languages (whether philologists admit a lineal connection is a matter of comparative indifference for periods so remote), suggest that the old rumbling, guttural 'r', which our modern palates have so thinned and refined, once had its concrete connection with swift, natural movements such as those of torrents or landslides.[1]

Now the conscious realization by men that such motions, with the noise that accompanies them, are often the prelude to disaster, may or may not have been the cause why 'ruo' came to convey in such a lively manner the notion, not only of movement, but also of *collapse*. If so, then we are already at the 'metaphorical' stage, and the transition from 'given' to 'created' meaning has begun, even before the first recorded use. If not, then an older single meaning ('rush-fall-collapse') has begun, under the influence of the rational, to split up into this treble meaning of the Latin word—which is subsequently going to require *three separate words* for its expression. In any case it is noticeable that, when the substantive 'ruina' came to be formed, it contained this last part only of the meaning of the verb—in other words, the older meaning, whether still wholly

[1] Boiardo, in the *Orlando Innamorato*, uses the Italian equivalent, on two consecutive pages, to express (i) a swiftly flowing river ('L'acqua che al corso una *rovina* pare') and (ii) a fall in battle:

> '*E ben credette d'averlo conquiso,*
> '*E* rovinarlo *a quel sol colpo al piano*'

while a few pages further on we find it (iii) describing a man galloping off on horseback:

> '*Allor ne andava lui con gran* rovina,
> '*Spronando il buon destriero a piu potere.*'

'given' or containing by now a 'created' element, was now being further restricted, hardened, *arrested*, under the influence of the rational principle. And another change soon took place: it could now mean, not only the falling itself, but *the thing fallen*. It is like watching a physical process of crystallization.

Guy de Maupassant said somewhere: 'Les mots ont une âme; la plupart des lecteurs, et même des écrivains, ne leur demandent qu'un sens. Il faut trouver cette âme qui apparaît au contact d'autres mots. . . .' It will, I think, appear that this 'soul', latent in words, and waiting only to be discovered, is for the most part a kind of buried survival of the old 'given' meaning under later accretions; or, if not of the 'given' meaning itself, then of an old 'created' meaning which has been buried in the same way. For created meanings, once published, are as much subject, of course, to the binding, astringent action of the rational principle as the original given meanings. Like sleeping beauties, they lie there prone and rigid in the walls of Castle Logic, waiting only for the kiss of Metaphor to awaken them to fresh life. That words lose their freshness through habit is a more humdrum way of saying the same thing; and it will do well enough, as long as we remember that 'habit' is itself only a familiar name for the repetition of the identical, and that the repetition of the identical is the very essence of the rational principle—the very means by which the concrete becomes abstract—the Gorgon's head itself.

The words 'au contact d'autres mots' (which remind us of the tag from the *Ars Poetica*: 'notum si callida verbum Reddiderit *iunctura* novum . . .') are particularly important.

For this 'contact' with other words is *the precise point at which the potential new meaning originally enters language.* And it is by quotations illustrating such 'contacts' that I am trying to trace the gradual loss of ancient meaning, given or created, from the word 'ruin', the recovery of part of it, and the positive gain which, thanks to individual poets, arises out of that sequence of loss and recovery.

In Latin, then, the four letters 'r-u-i-n' never lost the power to suggest *movement.* In certain contexts they may seem to modern readers to possess a purely static and material reference; but if so, it is because those readers are of the kind described by Maupassant as demanding only a 'sens', a definable meaning. The *soul* of such a word as 'ruina' is really inseparable from motion.

Si fractus illabatur orbis,
Impavidum ferient ruinae

says Horace; the world is still falling when the stanza ends.

[3]

Before 1375 the word *ruin* with the meaning 'a falling' has come, via France, to England, and we find Chaucer using it in that sense. Thus, Saturn, in the *Knight's Tale,* boasting of his powers, proclaims to Venus:

Min is the ruine of the highe halles,
The falling of the toures and of the walles.

Here is the word in poetic use, mobile and vigorous enough, but without its modern subtlety, because in English it has as yet no *solid* associations to give it weight and deepen its private significance. It is simply a useful Latin word. So, too, we may notice that Gower, about the same time, is employing the word almost in its exact classical sense:

The wal and al the cit withinne
Stant in ruine and in decas,

where we should now say 'stand in *ruins*', and think at once, not of a process or a state (which is Gower's meaning) but of the actual fragments of masonry.[1] 1454 is the date of the first recorded instance of plural use with a definitely material reference—*ruins*—and it is probable that by Spenser's time the meaning was quickly spreading over the special area which it was to cover during the eighteenth century. He writes, it is true:

The late ruin of proud Marinell,

meaning Marinell's disastrous defeat in battle, and uses the word twenty-one times in this older sense; but he also uses the modern plural thirteen times, and speaks of

The old ruines of a broken towre.

These two lines alone are enough to show that already, before the end of the sixteenth century, the English word, with the double set of associations which it was now beginning to acquire, had a 'soul'; though no one had quite found it; no one, that is, had realized it in consciousness. For it was not in the nature of English poetry before the seventeenth century to 'add' meaning to words in this way, by evoking their hidden quality. Thus, Spenser, who made all English into a language of his own, half-creating

[1] Cf. V, 2 and 3.

in his poesy another Spenserian world, which never quite touches the real one, gave little of *permanence* to language. As creator of language, Spenser was fantastic rather than imaginative.[1]

[4]

By this time, however, English meaning had suddenly begun to ferment and bubble furiously round about a brain in a Stratford cottage; witness the sheer verbal exuberance of *Love's Labour's Lost.* Many of its words were to suffer an extraordinary change before the century was out, however slowly that change might become apparent. In some cases the new energy in them was not to be released until the nineteenth century—even later. But the energy was there. There is a new English Dictionary hidden between the pages—or is it between the lines?—of the First Folio. Shakespeare stands supreme over the other poets of the world in the one great quality of abundant life; and this he gave to words, as he gave it to Falstaff and Sir Andrew Aguecheek. He made more new words than any other English writer—but he also made new meanings. We are at present concerned only with the word *ruin*; let us listen, then, to Salisbury's words, when he is confronted with Arthur's body lying huddled on the stones, where the fall has killed him:

It is the shameful work of Hubert's hand,
The practice and the purpose of the King;
From whose obedience I forbid my soul,
Kneeling before this ruin of sweet life . . .

[1] He seems, however, to have invented the useful epithet, *blatant*, though he himself never employed it outside the conventional title of the 'Blatant Beast'.

'Les mots ont une âme . . .' No synonym would do here; the phrase

Kneeling before this ruin of sweet life

is one—a tiny work of art. In Spenser's line

The late ruin of proud Marinell

you could substitute *fall* or *disaster*, if the syllables would scan. But Shakespeare has felt the exact, whole significance of his word. The dead boy has *fallen* from the walls; the sweet life, which was in him too, has crumbled away; but wait—by Shakespeare's time the word was beginning to acquire its other meaning of the actual remains—and there is the shattered body lying on the ground! He has, indeed, found a soul in the word.

It seems to have been one which appealed dearly to his imagination, for we find the transitive verb in one of the loveliest lines from the sonnets:

That time of year thou may'st in me behold
When yellow leaves, or none, or few do hang
Upon those boughs which shake against the cold,
Bare ruin'd choirs, where late the sweet birds sang.

But it was in *Antony and Cleopatra*, near the end of his work, that he made the boldest stroke of all, writing quietly but magnificently:

The noble ruin of her magic, Antony.

There is a new word. Yet Shakespeare had not done it *all* with his own hands. The transitive verb 'to ruin' had been invented already, by 1585, before he started to write, and, without the new habit of thought which this use of them was forming in himself *and in his hearers*, he could not have used the four letters passively with such effect. For a poet must take his words as he finds them, and his readers must not realize too acutely that fresh meaning is being thrust upon them. The new meaning must be *strange*, not incomprehensible; otherwise the poetry of the whole passage is killed, and the fresh meaning itself will be still-born.

[5]

The word *ruin*, then, has grown with Shakespeare's help into a warm and living thing, a rich piece of imaginative material ready at hand for anyone who has the skill to evoke its power. Now, early in the seventeenth century, it had been used for the first time as an intransitive verb, taking the place once and for all of an older verb, to *rue*, which had the same meaning, but never probably (since it had not been used by the poets) the same suggestive power. Grimstone, in a *History of the Siege of Ostend* (1604), wrote: 'They suffered it to burn and ruin'; while Sandys, in a verse paraphrase (!) of Job, has:

Though he his House of polisht marble build,
Yet shall it ruine like the Moth's fraile cell.

It was natural that Milton, with his bookish sense of the philological history of his words, should come forward to perpetuate this use. To the noun *ruin* he added nothing; what he did was to help 'fix' its Latinity by *never once* using it in its modern material sense. So that when Satan

yet shone, majestic though in Ruin,

he exerted only a negative, if deepening, influence on the history of the word. It is the terrific phrase:

> *Hell heard the insufferable noise, Hell saw*
> *Heaven ruining from Heaven*

which is important. For it is preserving that old content of large and disastrous movement, which Wordsworth, Milton's devout disciple, has finally recovered for us into the language.

But there is all the eighteenth century in between; and during that time *ruin*, like most words other than domestic and civic and scientific terms, seems to have possessed a greatly diminished power of suggestion. These latter words, of course, grew. Pope, for instance, found out a kind of soul in the word *engine*, when he used it in the *Rape of the Lock* of a pair of scissors:

> *He takes the gift with reverence, and extends*
> *The little engine on his fingers' ends.*

But the others—especially those purporting to be descriptive of Nature—must have felt uncomfortably stifled, and many of them, as we have seen, actually lost much of their poetic vitality. The question was, in each case, whether any poet would arise to restore it.

Dryden wrote:

> *So Helen wept, when her too faithful glass*
> *Reflected to her eyes the ruins of her face.*

But after that, until the coming of Wordsworth, it is all tumbledown walls and mossy masonry. We can just imagine how *solid* an idea must have been imprinted by the word *ruins* on an eighteenth-century imagination, and how faintly its original force must have survived, when we recollect the fashion of erecting artificial 'follies'. In this connection Dryden's own use of the plural rather than the singular is interesting, as emphasizing the solid, material reference of the meaning. Indeed, I believe that to his own fancy, as well as to those of many of his readers, the phrase was actually an 'accidental'[1] metaphor in which the lady's face was compared to the 'picturesque' remains of a Gothic abbey.

[6]

All this suggests a feature, to which attention has not yet been drawn, in the history of Poetic Diction, or rather in the parallel history of that anti-poetic process, which I have ventured to describe as the 'splitting up' of meaning, and which accompanies the natural decline of language into abstraction. It is this; that under certain circumstances, poets themselves may assist that process. Thus, the *first time* *ruin* was used alone with a blunt and, as it were, purely material, meaning, that use of it may have been original and poetic. The first man who looked at the ruin of a wall and called it simply a *ruin* may well have had the true dramatic-poetic sense of the value of *omission*, with its accompanying phenomenon of *suggestion*. It was this kind of omission, presumably, which gave to *bode* its dark prophetic significance. Just as the poetry of today, then, may have been but the normal language of yesterday, so, much that appears in the light of subsequent development to have been really, by its proper nature, in the prosaic stream, may

[1] See Appendix III.

yet have been true poetry to the experience of contemporaries. During the eighteenth century itself there may well have been a romance and a flavour clinging to their own favourite use of the word *ruin*—a romance not quite so false and a flavour not quite so insipid as we must think, whose only understanding of those different minds is derived from a language which has also changed.

[7]

Pope made no uncommon use of the word, nor added much to its power. Nor did anyone else. Nevertheless the word means more than it did before the eighteenth century had come and gone; for, from now on, it is irradiated with some of the massive quiet of deserted Gothic masonry. And no matter how many times it has been carelessly handled for the purposes of false and facile romanticism, the old magic will always be ready to flash out to a touch of true imagination.

So time passed. Young, it is true, had felt the quality of the word, and there may be other isolated examples. In the second book of the *Night Thoughts* the father is describing the appearance of his dead daughter lying stretched upon her bed:

Lovely in death the beauteous ruin lay.

It is a definite echo, I think, of the line from *King John*—a dying echo—and with Gray the soul of the word finally runs to seed in the fanciful, allegorical, synthetic dullness of actual personification:

Ruin seize thee, ruthless King!

Then came Wordsworth, who immediately, in one of his earliest poems, *The Descriptive Sketches*, got a move, as it were, on the word and dislodged it from its sentimental repose. He used it of an avalanche:

> *From age to age throughout his lonely bounds*
> *The crash of ruin fitfully resounds.*

And the verb neuter of a waterfall:

> *Ruining from the cliffs the deafening load*
> *Tumbles.*

We are back again now with Milton. Wordsworth has gone to the other extreme, and both these uses are a little too near to the word's simplest etymological significance, are not new enough to be very striking; yet doubtless at the time when they were written they had the power to startle. They are a clear enough symptom of that general quickening of perception which found its expression in the Romantic Revival. Hundreds of dead words might be resuscitated by men like Bishop Percy and Sir Walter Scott; it was the task of even more vital spirits to awaken those that were only sleeping.

It is doubtful whether Tennyson or Browning have added much—or perhaps it is too early to say. On the whole, Tennyson's tendency is to abstract the meaning from reality and semi-personify it:

> *When the crimson rolling eye*
> *Glares ruin!*

And again:

> *The Sea roars Ruin. A fearful night!*

Note the capital letter. And yet, in *Lucretius*, there is that one magnificent example of the verb neuter:

> *A void was made in Nature; all her bonds*
> *Crack'd; and I saw the flaring atom-streams*
> *And torrents of her myriad universe,*
> *Ruining along the illimitable inane . . .*

[8]

Here, then, is the modern word *ruin*—a piece of many lost minds—waiting, like all the other words in the dictionary, to be kindled into life by a living one; and nothing more is necessary than to surround it with other words (the right ones) from the same museum. Is this being done at all in contemporary verse? There is one line at least, written by a modern poet, which may be quoted. Some time ago, when I had finished reading a volume of verse by Mr. E. L. Davison, two passages remained to haunt me. Both of them contained the word *ruin*, and it was, as a matter of fact, this coincidence which first interested me in the word's poetic history. The first is from a poem called *The Sunken City*:

> *. . . the climbing tentacles*
> *Of some sleep-swimming octopus*
> *Disturb a ruined temple's bells*
> *And set the deep sea clamorous.*

Thus, the very choice of subject suggests that the poet's imagination is one which is attracted by the somewhat dangerous beauty of 'ruin'. So we find. Take these two lines from a love-sonnet in the same volume:

I stood before thee, calling twice or thrice
The ruin of thy soft, bewildering name.

In a way this line seems to be a summing up of all previous poetic uses of the word, and then a step beyond them: 'ruin' showers noiselessly over it in a kind of dream-waterfall of pangs.

In this chapter, I have taken only one English word, and one no richer in itself than a thousand others. Yet it serves well enough to show how the man of today, overburdened with self-consciousness, lonely, insulated from Reality by his shadowy, abstract thoughts, and ever on the verge of the awful maelstrom of his own fantastic dreams, has among his other compensations these lovely ancestral words, embalming the souls of many poets dead and gone and the souls of many common men. If he is a poet, he may rise for a moment on Shakespeare's shoulders—if he is a lover, then, certainly, there are no more philtres, but he has his four magical black squiggles, wherein the past is bottled, like an Arabian Genie, in the dark. Let him only find the secret, and there, lying on the page, their printed silence will be green with moss; it will crumble slowly even while it whispers with the thunder of primeval avalanches. 'Le mot', murmured Victor Hugo . . . 'tantôt comme un passant mystérieux de l'âme, tantôt comme un polype noir de l'océan pensê. . . .'

VIII

THE MAKING OF MEANING (II)

[1]

A very little practise in this method of concentration on the meaning of the single word will convince anyone who cares to try it of the insight which it brings into the beating heart of poetry. Nevertheless hardly any criticism along such lines has been attempted. As far as I know, Goldsmith's essay on *Poetry as Distinguished from Other Writing* is practically the first and last of its kind in English. In this essay Goldsmith took (among some other words) the Latin verb *pendere*, first quoting the observation of a previous critic that Virgil had frequently 'poetized' a whole sentence by means of the same word. He cited:

> *Ite meae, felix quondam pecus, ite capellae,*
> *Non ego vos posthac, viridi projectus in antro,*
> *Dumosa* pendere *procul de rupe videbo.*

and

> *Hi summo in fluctu* pendent, *his unda dehiscens*
> *Terram inter fluctus aperit;*

And, again, the description of Dido listening to Æneas:

Iliacos iterum demens audire labores
Exposcit, pendetque *iterum narrantis ab ore.*

And he went on to show how the English poets have carried on, or repeated, these delicate uses, quoting Shakespeare's

half way down
Hangs *one that gathers samphire—dreadful trade!*

Milton's description of Adam:

he, on his side,
Leaning half-raised, with looks of cordial love
Hung *over her enamoured.*

And Addison's

Thy providence my life sustained,
And all my wants redressed,
When in the silent womb I lay,
And hung *upon the breast.*

[2]

Goldsmith, however, said nothing of the light which this kind of criticism can be made to throw on the genius of the individual poet; and that is one of its most significant uses. At the same time it is much harder to exemplify; for its delicacy is apt to be lost in any attempt to restrain it within the strait-jacket of a prose description. It is rather for the reader himself to be ready to pull up and ponder when he is struck by a peculiar meaning. The author of a little book called *Milton and Metaphysics*, which appeared a few years ago, gave evidence that he had learnt some of

Coleridge's secrets by pausing in just this way on his distinctive uses of the word *quiet*; and Mr. Bonamy Dobrée, in his *Literary Biographies*, had a delightful appendix on Addison's curious love of *secret*.

One can readily find other examples. To allow oneself, for instance, to experience to the full the wealth of meaning which the little epithet *trim* contained for Milton, is to see the world through his eyes in a specially intimate way. From *Samson Agonistes* we see that he is aware of its nautical tang; for we find it in that wonderful description of Dalilah's approach:

> *But who is this, what thing of Sea or Land?*
> *Female of sex it seems,*
> *That so bedeckt, ornate, and gay,*
> *Comes this way sailing*
> *Like a stately Ship*
> *Of* Tarsus, *bound for th' Isles*
> *Of* Javan *or* Gadier
> *With all her bravery on, and tackle* trim,
> *Sails fill'd, and streamers waving. . . .*

It is the same whiff of fastidious tidiness, blown ashore, as it were, from some little cabin on the high seas, which gives to the 'trim gardens' of *Il Penseroso* their peculiar character:

> *And add to these retired Leasure,*
> *That in* trim *gardens takes his pleasure;*

We can almost feel the spotless linen of the dainty young scholar—demure without being effeminate—who is walking in them. And how specifically Miltonic is that landscape in *l'Allegro*—the unforgettable

Meadows trim, *with daisies pied.*

Or again, anyone who will trouble to get out a Shakespeare Concordance and dwell imaginatively on the number and variety of Shakespeare's uses of the word *function* (which is not found in our language at all until about fifty years before he began to write) cannot, I believe, fail to feel, with a new amazement, the creative working of his genius, and to feel it, *not merely by inference from its results*, but as taking a kind of part in the very process.

[3]

The coining of new words, as far as it is certainly attributable, is also a factor of some importance. That Shakespeare should apparently be the father of such everyday English words as *pedant*, *critic*, *majestic*, etc.; Dryden of the adjectives *mawkish* and *correct*; Coleridge of *pessimism*, *Elizabethan*, *dynamic*, *self-conscious*—even that Lord Chesterfield gave us *parsonical*—all this is interesting not only critically, but historically. It is interesting critically, when we notice the *kind* of word which this or that writer tends to create; historically, when we go on to consider how far any such word, as an embodiment of new meaning, was a substantial gift to the general consciousness. But I fancy it is easy to exaggerate the importance of these phenomena. They are more often etymological than semantic, and one must not, in the delight of finding something rather more tangible than the elusive 'change of meaning', allow oneself to forget that their significance is often little more than anecdotal. Meaning is everything. When we can experience a change of meaning—a *new* meaning—there we may really join hands and sing with the morning stars; for there we are in at the birth. There is one of the exact points at which the genius, the *originality*, of the individual poet has first entered the world.

[4]

The objection will possibly be raised that this dwelling upon the meanings of individual words is a precious and dilettante kind of criticism. But, as a matter of fact (sententious as it must sound) the reverse is the truth. Words whose meanings are relatively fixed and established, words which can be defined—words, that is, which are used with precisely the same connotation by different speakers—are *results*, they are *things become*. The arrangement and rearrangement of such univocal terms in a series of propositions is the function of *logic*, whose object is elucidation and the elimination of error. The poetic has nothing to do with this. It can only manifest itself as *fresh meaning*; it operates essentially *within* the individual term, which it creates and recreates by the magic of new combinations. Horace chose his *iunctura*, and Maupassant his *contact*, well: for in the pure heat of poetic expression juxtaposition is far more important than either logic or grammar. Thus, the poet's relation to terms is that of maker.[1] And it is in this making of terms—whether the results are to be durable or

[1] The *use* of them is left to the Logician, who, in his endeavour to keep them steady and thus fit them to his laws, is continually seeking to *reduce* their meaning. I say seeking to do so, because logic is essentially a compromise. He could only evolve a language, whose propositions would *really* obey the laws of thought by eliminating meaning altogether. But he compromises before this zero-point is reached. See also VII, I, note.

fleeting—that we can divine the very poetic itself. When we strive to contemplate the genesis of meaning—to be one with the poet, as it were, while the term is still uncreate—then we have descended with Faust into the realm of the Mothers; then we are drinking of the springs and freshets of Becoming.

Surely, if criticism is anything worth while, it must be a sort of midwifery—not, of course, in the Socratic sense, but retrospectively. It must try to alter the state of mind of the artist's audience, from mere wondering contemplation of an inexplicable *result*, towards something more like sympathetic participation in a process. And in poetry, as far as it is merely semantic, and not dramatic, or sentimental, or musical—this process is the making of meaning. What kind of criticism, then, is dilettante: that which attempts to know, by sharing in, the poetic process itself, or the fastidious sort which can only moon aimlessly about the room with its hands in its pockets, till the infant is nicely washed and dried and ready for inspection?

There is really no end to the secrets hidden behind the meanings of single words—though I do not suggest that meditation on such meanings is the *only* way to come by them. Nevertheless, wherever two consciousnesses differ, as it were, in kind, and not merely in relative lucidity—there the problem of sympathy can always be narrowed down to the problem of the meaning of some one or more fundamental words. One of the most striking examples of this truth is the interpretation of Greek philosophy by modern Europeans. Such an one can read Plato and Aristotle through from end to end, he can even write books expounding their philosophy, and all without understanding a single sentence. Unless he has enough imagination, and enough power of detachment from the established meanings or thought-forms of his own civilization, to enable him to grasp the meanings of the fundamental terms —unless, in fact, he has the power not only of thinking, but of *unthinking*—he will simply re-interpret everything they say in terms of subsequent thought. If he merely seeks to deduce the meaning of words like ἄρχη, λόγος, γίγνομαι, ψύχη, δύναμις from the general context, if he cannot rather *feel* the way in which they *came into being out of the essential nature of the Greek consciousness as a whole*, he may read pages and pages of Greek letterpress, and enjoy them, but he will know no more than the shadow of Greek meaning. One could add many other words, but it would take us too far afield. Spengler is excellent on the untranslatableness of these 'root-words', as he calls them, and in insisting on the consequently unbridgeable gap between the souls of any two great cultures.

But if these words are really quite untranslatable, if the gulf is truly unbridgeable, it will be said—what is the use of talking about them? The answer to this is that the meaning of such words—like all strange meaning—while not expressible in definitions and the like (the prosaic), *is* indirectly expressible in metaphor and simile (the poetic). That is to say, it is suggestible; for meaning itself can never be *conveyed* from one person to another; words are not bottles; every individual must intuit meaning for himself, and the function of the poetic is to mediate such intuition by suitable suggestion.

A book appeared recently called *The Meaning of Meaning*. The authors of this work wrote on page 5 (in a brief critique of M. Bréal's *Semantics*) that 'it is impossible thus to handle a scientific matter in metaphorical terms'. The reader is thus confronted with a long and clever book on Meaning, the authors of which have never managed to grasp its essential feature—the relation to metaphor. How did this come about? The book would certainly never have been written, if they had started their theory of Meaning from the only possible starting-point—the meaningless. But, instead of this, they have taken as jumping-off place one particular, highly elaborated system of meanings, which they apparently regard as being in some way fundamental. The book is thus a painful example of the *lack* of just that power of detachment from the thought-forms of a particular civilization, to which I have referred. The authors of *The Meaning of Meaning* have never practised the gentle art of *unthinking*, though it is one for which the subtlety and agility of their intellects must, as a matter of fact, make them peculiarly fitted. As a result, they are absolutely rigid under the spell of those verbal ghosts of the physical sciences, which today make up practically the whole meaning-system of so many European minds. This may seem a strong expression; yet surely nothing but a kind of enchantment could have prevented two intelligent people who had succeeded in writing a treatise some four hundred pages long on the 'meaning of meaning', from realizing that linguistic symbols have a *figurative* origin; a rule from which high-sounding 'scientific' terms like *cause*, *reference*, *organism*, *stimulus*, etc., are not miraculously exempt! That those who profess to eschew figurative expressions are really confining themselves to one very old kind of figure, might well escape the ordinary psychological or historical writer; it usually does; that it should escape the specialist in Meaning is somehow horribly tragic. And indeed the book is a ghastly tissue of empty abstractions.

[5]

It will be remembered that, as I am using the terms, a word has a 'figurative' origin in so far as its meaning is 'given' in the sense developed in IV, 3 and VI, 1; a 'metaphorical' origin, in so far as its meaning is the product of the inventive constructions of individuals. Now a great deal—perhaps most—of the technical vocabularly of philosophy and science can be shown to be not merely figurative, but actually metaphorical.

It will also be plain by this time that I have been using the word 'poet'in the wide sense beloved of the Romatics—the sense in which, as Shelley put it, 'Plato was a poet, Lord Bacon was a poet'. The literary justification of this use will be considered in the next chapter. Before passing on, however, it may be useful to point to some groups of common words, in which this 'making of meaning' is historically perceptible and has indeed had effects reaching far outside the domain of literature.

Coleridge's *point of view* has already been cited. His novel use of the word *imagination*—distinguishing it from *fancy*—is another example of the introduction of fresh meaning into the English language. Similarly, a careful study of Shakespeare reveals him as the probable author of a great part of the *modern* meanings of several words which are practically key-terms to whole areas of typical modern thought—especially to those parts of it which are peculiarly the discovery of English thinkers. He was, for example, as far as is known to the compilers of the *Oxford Dictionary*, the first person to use *function* of a physical organ, and the first person to use *inherit*, not of property, but of moral or physical qualities.[1] *Nerve* meant a sinew or tendon, or, metaphorically, strength, before he employed it in its modern physical sense; and the word *voluntary* is not known to have been applied to human actions—except with a definite connotation of moral disapproval—until it was so applied in Shakespeare's works. He is also the first writer quoted in the *Oxford Dictionary* as applying the words *create*, *adore*, *religion*, *magic*, to other than avowedly supernatural or (in the case of *adore*) royal subjects.

These are only a few examples of the effect of Shakespeare's genius on what I ventured to call in the last chapter 'English meaning'. Exactly how far it has reverberated outside England into modern consciousness as a whole is a question into which I cannot enter here. But no one with any delicacy of historical insight can fail to connect much in the consciousness—outlook—experience of life, or whatever we choose to call it—of modern Europe as a whole with, for instance, that change of attitude which is reflected in the transfer of Latin-French devotional words such as *anguish*, *bounty*, *mercy*, *comfort*, *compassion*, *devotion*, *grace*, *passion*, etc., to secular contexts. This transference can actually be watched in the development of medieval verse, until the new attitude receives its final expressive stamp at the hands of the Elizabethans. Oscar Wilde's *mot*—that men are made by books rather than books by men—was

[1] *Heredity*, as a definite name for the principle by which like begets like, is not found till 1863.

certainly not pure nonsense; there is a very real sense, humiliating as it may seem, in which what we generally venture to call *our* feelings are really Shakespeare's 'meaning'.

It would be possible to carry these considerations farther back—to inquire, for example, how far the meanings of such metaphysical key-words as *absolute*, *cause*, *concept*, *essence*, *intuition*, *potential*, *matter*, *form*, *objective*, *subjective*, *ideal*, *general*, *special*, *individual*, *universal*, are merely figurative, and how far they are metaphorical in the sense of having been contributed by individual philosophers whether Greek, medieval, or modern. In some cases a radical change can be detected in quite recent times. *Subjective*, from signifying 'existing in itself', came during the seventeenth century to signify 'existing *only* in human consciousness'.[1]

Again, that expression of nature as a system of laws, which is commonly implied today when the word 'science' is used, has played its vital part in the development of modern meaning. And owing to the necessarily[2] late period at which the possibility of seeing nature in this light arises, it may safely be said that *all* meanings of this kind are metaphorical rather than figurative. In many cases the original metaphorical use can be quite probably identified. Thus, it would seem that we owe to Bacon the application of *mechanical* to natural principles. The important change

[1] For a detailed scrutiny of the history of these terms the reader is referred to Rudolf Eucken's *Geschichte der Philosophischen Terminologie*. A more general and superficial survey of semantic development has been attempted in the author's *History in English Words*.

[2] Because it demands an advanced stage of self-consciousness, and is in general a characteristic of the prosaic.

of meaning introduced about Newton's time into the words *gravity* and *gravitation*, which had previously meant 'weight' and 'falling', will be familiar to everyone. And Kepler's metaphorical use of the Latin *focus* (a hearth) in a geometrical context, and its subsequent introduction into the English language by Hobbes must mark an important step in the development of that modern *relational* mathematics, which Spengler has shown so convincingly to be a peculiar manifestation of Western consciousness, and which has had such important results outside of mathematics. To his book, and to the Appendices at the end of this one, I would refer those who may object that what I am calling 'the development of meaning' is simply a confusing name for the discovery of fact.

[6]

When we start explaining the language of famous scientists as examples of 'poetic diction', it may well seem that the ordinary meaning of that literary phrase has been inflated beyond the bounds of reason. Nevertheless such an extension was necessary, in order to make clear its real nature. Nor has it been waste of time, if it has convinced a single person who needed convincing, how essentially parochial is the fashionable distinction between Poetry and Science as modes of experience.

It has already been emphasized that the rational principle must be strongly developed in the great poet. Is it necessary to add to this that the scientist, if he has 'discovered' anything, must also have discovered it by the right interaction of the rational and poetic principles? Really, there is no distinction between Poetry and Science, as kinds of knowing, at all. There is only a distinction between bad poetry and bad science. That the two or three experimental sciences, and the two or three hundred specialized lines of inquiry which ape their methods, should have developed the rational out of all proportion to the poetic is indeed an historical fact—and a fact of great importance to a consideration of the last four hundred years of European history. But to imagine that this tells us anything about the *nature* of knowledge; to speak of method as though it were a way of knowing instead of a way of testing, this is—instead of looking dispassionately *at* the historical fact—to wear it like a pair of blinkers.

If we must have a fundamental dichotomy, how much more real it is (though even this is properly a division of function rather than of person) to divide man as knower from man in his other capacity as doer. Then, as knower, we shall find that he always knows by the interaction within himself of these poetic (ποιητικός) and logistic principles; and so we can divide him again, according to which of the principles predominates. If the poetic is unduly ascendant, behold the mystic or the madman, unable to grasp the reality of percepts at all—a being still resting, as it were, in the bosom of gods or demons—not yet man, man in the fullness of his stature, at all. But if the passive, logistic, prosaic principle predominates, then the man becomes—what? the *collector*, the man who cannot grasp the reality of anything *but* percepts. And here at last a real distinction between poet and scientist, or rather between poetaster and pedant, does arise. For if the 'collector's' interests happen to be artistic or literary, he will become the connoisseur, that is, he will collect either *objets d'art* or elegant sensations and memories. But if they are 'scientific', he will collect—data; will, in fact, probably go on doing so all his life, to the tune of solemn warnings against the formation of 'premature syntheses'.

That the idea of Poetry and Science as two fundamentally opposite modes of experiencing Life should have taken firm hold of a generation which honours Aristotle, Bacon and Goethe, will, I believe, be as much a matter of wonder to our posterity as it will—if not re-adjusted—be a matter of tragedy to ourselves. This is not the place to consider the effects of such an attitude on ordinary research, except as that can be seen through its effects on art. Alas, the latter are already palpable. For it leads straight to that Crocean conception of art as meaningless emotion—as *personal* emotion symbolized—which is so poisonous in its charter to all kinds of posturing and conceited egotism. No reflection is intended on Croce himself, whose works possess an extraordinarily selfless dignity; but that does not alter the fact that the spread of such a conception is a serious matter for a civilization which must look more and more to art—to the individualized poetic—as the very source and fountain-head of all meaning.

[7]

Provided, then, that we do not look too far back into the past (i.e. beyond the point at which the 'given' meaning of a word first began to yield place to the 'created' meaning) language does indeed appear historically as an endless process of metaphor transforming itself into meaning. Seeking for material in which to incarnate its last inspiration, imagination seizes on a suitable word or phrase, uses it as a metaphor, and so creates a meaning. The progress is from Meaning, through inspiration to imagination, and from imagination, through metaphor, to meaning; inspiration grasping the hitherto unapprehended, and imagination relating it to the already known.

Now it has been pointed out by others before this that there is no other way by which real *knowledge* of Nature can spread and increase—by which the consciousness of humanity can actually be enlarged, and knowledge, which is at present new and private, made public, but some form of metaphor. Bacon himself, than whom no one can ever have been more alive to the dangers of a vague and misty imagery (the very *idola theatri* which he had set out to smash), took the trouble to say so in the *Advancement of Learning*:[1]

'For that knowledge which is new, and foreign from opinions received, is to be delivered in another form than that that is agreeable and familiar; and therefore Aristotle, when he thinks to tax Democritus, doth in truth commend him, where he saith, *If we shall indeed dispute, and not follow after similitudes*, etc. For those whose conceits are seated in popular opinions, need only but to prove or dispute; but

[1] II, xvii. 10. Aristotle too, however, when he came to think on the subject of poetry, seems to have realized the epistemological significance of metaphor. For he says in the *Poetics*; πολὺ μέγιστον τὸ μεταφορικόν. μόνον γὰρ τοῦτο οὔτε παρ' ἄλλου ἔστι λαβεῖν εὐφυιᾶς τε σημεῖον ἔστι. τὸ γὰρ εὖ μεταφέρειν τὸ τὸ ὅμοιον θεωρεῖν ἐστίν.

'The making of metaphors is by far the most important; since this alone does not involve borrowing from somebody else and is [therefore] a mark of genius; for to make a good metaphor is to contemplate likeness.

those whose conceits are beyond popular opinions, have a double labour: the one to make themselves conceived, and the other to prove and demonstrate. So that it is of necessity with them to have recourse to similitudes and translations to express themselves. And therefore in the infancy of learning, and in rude times when those conceits which are now trivial were then new, the world was full of parables and similitudes.'

So, also, today, Professor Baldwin in his *Thought and Things*,[1] points out how

'the development of thought . . . is by a method essentially of trial and error, of experimentation, *of the use of meanings as worth more than they are as yet recognized to be worth.* The individual must use his own thoughts, his established knowledges, his grounded judgements, for the embodiment of his new inventive constructions. He erects his thought as we say "schematically" . . . projecting into the world an opinion still peculiar to himself, as if it were true. *Thus all discovery proceeds.*'

Indeed, it was just their clear, even delighted, vision of this truth, which misled the more imaginative philologists into the errors I discussed in the chapter on *Metaphor*. So dazzled were they, that they fancied the same process must needs be true of *all* poetry, of *all* language, of *all* time. They failed to distinguish the poetic from the individualized poetic; they did not see that the creation of metaphor can only be predicated of a community in which the prosaic is already flourishing. Yet it is only by means of this prosaic spirit that the separate perceptual groups

[1] *Thought and Things*, II, p. 146

('phenomena'), which metaphor is to combine or relate, could ever have *become* separate. Moreover, it is only by means of this same principle that the individual consciousnesses, which are assumed to have done the creating, could ever have come into being. For the rational principle, the τὸ λογίζειν, is above all that which produces self-consciousness. It shuts off the human ego from the living meaning in the outer world, which it is for ever 'murdering to dissect', and encloses that same ego in the network of its own, now abstract, thoughts. And it is just in the course of that very shutting off that the ego itself stirs and awakes to conscious existence.

Yet, having awoken, it is as helpless as any other new-born thing without the life of the mother-Nature from which it sprang. Let the weaning be followed too soon by separation, and the wailing creature perishes of cold. Such a separation, a separation of consciousness from the real world, is today only too conspicuous alike in philosophy, science, literature, and normal experience. Isolated thus, suspended, as it were, *in vacuo*, and hermetically sealed from truth and life, not only the proper name, but the very ego itself, of which that is but the symbol, pines and dwindles away before our eyes to a thin nothing—a mere inductive abstraction from tabulated card-indexed behaviour, whose causes lie elsewhere. Nor is there any remedy for this state of affairs but that experience of truth, or identification of the self with the meaning of Life, which is both poetry and knowledge.

Now although, without the rational principle, neither truth nor knowledge could ever have been, but only Life itself, yet that principle alone cannot add one iota to knowledge. It can clear up obscurities, it can measure and enumerate with greater and ever greater precision, it can preserve us in the dignity and responsibility of our individual existences. But in no sense can it be said (cf. II, 5 and 6) to *expand* consciousness. Only the poetic can do this: only poesy, pouring into language its creative intuitions, can preserve its living meaning and prevent it from crystallizing into a kind of algebra. 'If it were not for the Poetic or Prophetic character,' wrote William Blake, 'the philosophic and experimental would soon be at the ratio of all things, and stand still, unable to do other than repeat the same dull round.' Like some others of the mystics, he had grasped without much difficulty the essential nature of meaning. For all meaning flows from the creative principle, the τὸ ποιεῖν, whether it lives on, as given and remembered, or is re-introduced by the individualized creative faculty, the analogy-perceiving, metaphor-making imagination. In Platonic terms we should say that the rational principle can increase *understanding*, and it can increase *true opinion*, but it can never increase *knowledge*. And herein is revealed the levity of chanting with too indiscriminate praises the triumphal 'progress' of our language from Europe to Cathay.

IX

VERSE AND PROSE

[1]

At the opposite pole to the wide sense in which I have been using the phrase 'poetic diction', stands the narrowest one, according to which it signifies 'language which can be used in verse but not in prose'. This artificial identification of the words *poetry* and *poetic* with metrical form is certainly of long standing in popular use; but it has rarely been supported by those who have written on the subject.[1] As *Verse* is an excellent word for metrical writing of all kinds, whether poetic or unpoetic, and *Prose* for un-metrical writing, in this book the formal literary distinction is drawn between *verse* and *prose*; whereas that between *poetry*, *poetic* on the one hand and *prosaic* on the other is a spiritual one, not confined to literature. The meanings which I attach to these latter words should already be fairly clear from the foregoing chapters. I will, however, add four definite examples:

(i)

On the roof
Of an itinerant vehicle I sate
With vulgar men about me . . .

is *verse*, and at the same time *prosaic*.

[1] Hegel, in his *Philosophy of Fine Art*, makes a notable exception

(ii) *The crows and choughs that wing the midway air*
Show scarce so gross as beetles; half way down
Hangs one that gathers samphire, dreadful trade!
Methinks he seems no bigger than his head.

is *verse* and at the same time *poetry*.

(iii) *I told the butcher to leave two and a half pounds of best topside.*

is *prose* and at the same time *prosaic*.

(iv) *Behold now this vast city, a city of refuge . . .* (Example vi)

is *prose* and at the same time *poetry* or *poetic*.

But if those writers who have seriously set out to discuss and define poetry have very rarely made metre their criterion, yet, *for historical reasons*, most of the poetry with which they have actually had to deal has, in fact, been in metrical form; and it is this, in all probability, which has given rise to the terminological confusion.

All literatures are, in their infancy, metrical, that is to say, based on a more or less regularly recurring rhythm. Thus, unless we wish to indulge all sorts of fanciful and highly 'logomorphic' notions,[1] we are obliged to assume that the earliest verse-rhythms were 'given' by Nature in the same way as the earliest 'meaning'. And this is comprehensible enough. Nature herself is perpetually rhythmic. Just as the myths still live on a ghostly life as fables after they have died as real meaning, so the old rhythmic human consciousness of Nature (it should rather be called

[1] e.g. That, before the invention of writing, metrical form was deliberately adopted as an aid to memory.

a *participation* than a consciousness) lives on as the tradition of metrical form. We can only understand the origin of metre by going back to the ages when men were conscious, not merely in their heads, but in the beating of their hearts[1] and the pulsing of their blood—when thinking was not merely *of* Nature, but was Nature herself.

It is only at a later stage that prose (=not-verse) comes naturally into being out of the growth of that rational principle which, with its sense-bound, abstract thoughts, divorces man's consciousness from the life of Nature. In our own language, for example, it is only during the last three centuries that there has grown up any considerable body of prose, on which the critic could work. Consequently, the derivation from *prose* (=not-verse) of the adjective *prosaic* (=not-poetic) is not accidental. On the contrary, it is a record of certain historical facts. And yet we are wrong if we deduce from it the apparently logical conclusion that not-verse=not-poetry. Why? The question can only be answered historically, and in connection with other questions, such as that which has just been discussed, of the responsibility of individuals for poetic values.

[2]

The time at which the prose form (or lack of form) first begins to be used as a vehicle for imaginative writing in any particular language would indeed call for a full treatment in the poet's history of language which I envisaged above. Such a history would no doubt consider to what

[1] Cf. IV, I.

extent it tended to coincide with that period of a balance, as it were, between the two principles, which seems to make a language ripe for the appearance of its great poet—the period when Italy produces her Dante, England her Shakespeare.[1] I do not myself feel competent to carry this inquiry further than to point out that in this country—though Malory had written poetic prose a century before—it was, in fact, shortly before the time of Shakespeare that serious experiments were first made with prose as an imaginative medium.

Certainly it could be shown, without difficulty, and from many different sides, how the rise of prose, whatever else it may signify, is a necessary event in the biography of a language developing along the lines traced out above. For instance, the increasing fixity of word-order has already been referred to, and this is obviously a factor which encourages the prose form for all kinds of writing. In such a line as Shelley's:

The wise want power: the powerful goodness want

we can feel only too acutely the kind of syntactical stiffness which tempts a modern poet to write in prose. Moreover, the late Sir Walter Raleigh did well to point out, apropos of Wordsworth's theory of poetic diction, that some of the flattest passages in that poet's own work are due to his having observed the *prose choice* of words (in accordance with his theory) without at the same time keeping to the natural *prose order*. The meaning of these phrases, the 'prose choice of words' and the 'prose order', implying, as they do, that there is also a poetic choice of words and a poetic

[1] V.3.

order, can be better considered in the next chapter. Meanwhile one may again recall Coleridge's definition of poetry as 'the best words in the best order'.

It is evident without further examples that *ceteris paribus*, where a rigidly regular metrical framework has to be applied to a language in which grammar is itself growing strict concerning the order in which words may be placed, it must become harder and harder for verse and poetry to keep house together. Nor is it without significance that we, today, should be more disgusted by 'inversions' of the kind quoted above, and consequently more afraid of them, than our immediate ancestors; as a glance at contemporary verse will prove beyond dispute.

Thus, if we chose to confine our prophetic gaze to language and its 'progress', we should certainly behold Poetry giving poor Verse a bill of divorce and flying at some distant date into the arms of prose. A study of Chinese literature, in which word-order, as has been pointed out, is already rigidly determinate and of paramount denotative importance, might possibly throw a more comforting light on this prospect—comforting, that is, to those whose ears delight especially in the rhythms and music of verse.[1] But, in any case, if we try to alter the focus of our vision and look upon the art of poetry as a whole, we shall find plenty of contradictory evidence. Such an attempt I cannot very well make, since it is my object to confine this book to that area of Poetry which is related to the intrinsic nature of

[1] As far, however, as analogies with our own tongue are concerned, it must be remembered that the language of China has apparently remained almost unchanged throughout the whole known period of her history; so that its evolution from a looser, more flexional, form is no more than a hypothesis, albeit a highly convincing one.

language. Thus, I ignore altogether such questions as dramatic or architectonic values, quality of personal emotion, etc.; even the element of rhythm can only by discussed in so far as it is found to be inseparable from the use of speech; and I can hardly touch upon the nature of *music*.

When the individual's part in the making of poetry has reached a point at which poetry becomes an 'art', an entirely new set of forces begins to break through the shell of language proper, forces which tend to increase rather than diminish with the further passing of time. These forces are, as we saw, imparted by the individual poet himself; and one of the moulds into which they flow is the *music* of poetry. Music (if one can use a fraction here) may comprise perhaps as much as half the *meaning* of a modern lyric. But here I merely wish to point to it as one of the factors which counterbalance the tendency towards the prose form which has just been traced. Music may be distinguished from rhythm by the increasing aesthetic value of *sound*, as against mere *time*, and, unlike rhythm, it is not an instinctive element in early speech. As the Aryan languages develop, the *quantitative* values, which gave a rhythm to some extent inherent in the language itself, decay, while *accent*, which is much more *a determination of the material part of language by the speaker's own peculiar meaning*, arises in their stead. Now the decay of the quantitative values leaves us with prose, but, on the other hand, the rise of accent brings us—music. Alliteration and assonance are discovered—both practically unknown[1] to the ancients—and if these are musical devices not wholly peculiar to verse, but open

[1] Deliberate onomatopoea can safely be distinguished from pure alliteration and assonance, whose end is music before imitation.

also to poetic prose, yet in rhyme we are face to face with the development, at a comparatively late date, of an entirely new system of versification.

The significance of rhyme to the history and making of poetry I consider to be outside the scope of this book; but the mere fact that such a form has come into being, *since* poetry was an art, may well remind us how much, how very much, is possible to the human imagination, once it has begun to drink, with fuller consciousness, from the primal source of Meaning. It would be pure fantasy to attempt to prescribe in advance what uses man himself shall henceforth make of the material element in language.

X

ARCHAISM

[1]

At the beginning of this book it was found that poetic pleasure—the stir of aesthetic imagination—is caused by a change of consciousness from one level to another. And, in what followed, we saw that, while such a change can be brought about by all sorts of means, yet, within the bounds of a study of language itself, the one most constantly operative is the lapse of time. For the natural progress of language, if left, as it were, to itself, is a progress from poetic towards prosaic. It thus tends to bring about conditions suitable for appreciation, such appreciation being no other than when an unconsciously created meaning (the poetic in language and experience) is realized, or *finds* itself, in full waking consciousness—which latter state is itself made possible by the prosaic principle. It is not surprising, therefore, to find that the most characteristic phenomena of poetic diction, the most typical differences between the language of poetry and prosaic language, can be grouped under the heading of Archaism.

'The language of the age', wrote Gray, 'is never the language of poetry, except among the French, whose verse, where the thought or image does not support it, differs in nothing from prose.' And the late Sir Walter Raleigh went so far as to say that the language of poetry *always* has 'a certain archaic flavour'. Indeed, to the average person, the phrase 'poetic diction' is probably almost synonymous with what the literary mean by 'Archaism'. Much that might seem to claim separate treatment will be found, on analysis, to come within reach of this general principle; even the verse-form, for instance, which, though not essential, still remains one of the most constant empirical distinctions between poetry and the prosaic, is, from one point of view, a kind of archaism, as we saw in the last chapter. Again, if we truly understand the normal progress of language, the poet's distaste for 'abstract' words and his preference for the 'concrete', his distaste for subordination and his love of main sentences, fall equally smoothly into line.

[2]

Dismissing versification, which has already received separate treatment, we can divide the ground covered by archaism in poetic diction into two principal parts—Choice of Words, and Grammar. Let us consider the latter first: 'The most subtle form of archaism', says M. Bréal, in his *Semantics*, 'is to appeal to grammatical methods that no longer exist in the popular consciousness.' Now the epithet 'subtle' here is somewhat restrictive; it suggests the archaism of the delicate scholar who mobilizes all sorts of refined literary associations to tickle the fancies of persons similarly educated, and of those persons only. It suggests, in fact, the allusive style in which Milton excelled, and which is indeed *one* of the forms of grammatical archaism. Thus, to take the full savour of

> *Me miserable! which way shall I flie*
> *Infinite wrauth, and infinite despaire?*
> *Which way I flie is Hell; myself am Hell....*

one must be acquainted, not so much with the earlier habit of one's own tongue, as with something more recondite still—a dead language.

But outside this deliberate archaism, consciously aiming at a special effect, there are all those numberless little peculiarities of poetic diction, such as (in English) the use of the second person singular, verb-endings in *-eth* and old strong aorists like *clomb*, *drave*, etc., or the double negative, which the poet uses instinctively rather than of set purpose, and which, provided the poetic level of his work is sufficiently sustained, will pass practically unnoticed. That this traditional right to archaic expression should have grown up in the poetry of most nations is more than comprehensible, it appears as almost inevitable in the light of the foregoing principles. For we have seen how, in the Aryan group of languages, grammar grows more and more logical, more and more adapted to the concise expression of abstract thought, and, conversely, less fit for the embodiment of meaning which has not yet become abstract, and therefore eludes logical confinement. Thus, a dilemma which is inherent in all poetic expression is intensified for the modern poet by modern grammar.

'Much of our poetry' [wrote the late Henry Bradley] 'is obscure on a first reading, not because the diction is affected or allusive, but because the structure of the language has compelled the poet to choose between the claims of lucidity and those of emphasis or grace. There are passages in many English poets which are puzzling even to mature readers, but which if rendered literally into Latin or German would appear quite simple and straightforward.'[1]

(It should be remembered that in the progress of grammar, traced out in a previous chapter on the lines indicated by Professor Jespersen, English stands at a later stage than German.) And it is very easy to find examples which bear out Dr. Bradley's contention:

Music, when soft voices die,
Vibrates in the memory;
Odours, when sweet violets sicken,
Live within the sense they quicken.

Rose leaves, when the rose is dead,
Are heap'd for the belovèd's bed;
And so thy thoughts, when thou art gone,
Love itself shall slumber on.

How much would be gained here if either *thoughts* or *love* had, as in Latin, an accusative inflexion different in form from the nominative, or if the verb *shall* had a plural number, so that one could see at a glance which was subject and which object!

The English poet (and in varying degrees all modern European poets), faced with this unpleasant necessity of choosing between 'lucidity' and 'emphasis or grace'—which latter is, of course, another name for their proper poetic *meaning*—are acting perfectly in accord with the

[1] *The Making of English*, p. 73.

nature of language when they look where they do for a mode of expression in which there is more chance of combining the two. For since this hardening, as it were, of grammatical structure is not only noticeable as between one Aryan tongue and another, but is also operative in the biography of a single language, it is inevitable that they should lag behind in their choice of grammatical forms. It was again Henry Bradley who pointed out that 'the increased precision of modern English, though it is a great gain for the purposes of matter-of-fact statement, is sometimes the reverse of an advantage for the language of emotion and contemplation. Hence we find that our poetry, and our higher literature in general, often returns to the less developed grammar of the Elizabethan age.'[1]

And perhaps the most important element of all in this grammatical archaism is the extra liberty which the poet retains as to the *order* in which he shall arrange his words. This has been partly remarked already, and the causes are evident in the evolutionary tendency of speech towards a more and more crystallized, a more and more *Chinese*, condition. 'Poetry', says M. Bréal, 'has kept the habit of inversions, which are nothing but a licence of ancient days.' What innumerable examples of that familiar licence there are!—inversions which would be unthinkable in prosaic writing, and yet hardly strike the ear at all in poetry—of which, indeed, one is almost astonished to have it pointed out that they *are* inversions. What, for instance, could sound more simple, straight-forward, and modern than

Now sleeps the crimson petal, now the white,?

[1] *Ibid.*, p. 73.

But though M. Bréal has allowed himself to use the expression 'nothing but', it seems to me that there *is* another kind of inversion, one which is not simply a licence of ancient days retained instinctively for convenience, but is employed with set purpose to obtain a definite effect. Of such a kind, surely, is Milton's

Teiresias and Phineus, prophets old.

Of such a kind *par excellence* are the extraordinary inversions employed today with such conspicuous success by Walter de la Mare:

In mute desire she sways softly;
Thrilling sap up-flows;
She praises God in her beauty and grace,
Whispers delight. And there flows
A delicate wind from the Southern seas,
Kissing her leaves. She sighs.
While the birds in her tresses make merry;
Burns the sun in the skies.

It is fairly clear that the expressive significance of such inversions lies principally in the domain of *music* and is thus outside our scope. But it may be as well to point out that, while they are not mere archaic licences but, on the contrary, employed for special effects, yet even so they do not seem to be wholly divorced from the ancient habit of the language. To my ear at least there is in the poetry of de la Mare, especially in his habit of beginning the line with the main verb, a decided echo of the old alliterative measure which our modern metres have replaced—the earliest English verse. Nor is this surprising: the very fact that his rhythms have high poetic value should now suggest to us that the poet, while creating anew, is likely to be in a sense restoring something old. And if the most ancient rhythms of verse are but the sound, dying away, of just those 'footsteps of Nature' whose visible print we have observed, with Bacon, in the present possibility of true metaphor, we shall hardly be surprised to hear in the music which such a poet creates, albeit spontaneously, something like an echo of just those rhythms.

[3]

But if there is a difference between the prose order of words and the poetic order, there is also, as we saw, a prosaic and poetic *choice* of words. And it is here that archaism is often at the same time least conspicuous and most significant. Before considering in greater detail what may determine this poetic choice of words, it will be well to define archaism itself a little more narrowly; for confusion is only too easy, and much that may appear at first sight to be archaic is really nothing of the sort. Thus, the mere confining of oneself to a choice of words, a grammar or a set of mannerisms which has been for some time and is still in general literary use, is not archaism, though archaism may seem in the long run (and especially in the case of grammar) to involve that. This should merely be called *conservatism*, or even—not to put too fine a point on it—*dullness*. And its cause lies, not in the nature of language, but in the nature of man, and especially of literary man.

To say that conservatism in poetic diction is due to imitation is not to accuse those minor poets to whom it is due either of insincerity or of the lack of all genuine poetic experience. Charles Lamb, himself a minor poet, when solemnly told that he must 'write for the age', is said to have replied: 'Confound the age! I will write for antiquity!' If so, his gentle humour was giving a sort of intuitively correct expression to a fact in the history of literature. It was stated more exactly by Sir Walter Raleigh, when he said that poets 'learn from other poets'—not from conversation, as the prose-writer so often does. In this sense, Milton was a pupil of Spenser, and Pope and Wordsworth of Milton; but the result is not always as happy as in these cases. For a certain kind of pupil—as though more concerned to please his master than to digest his lesson—insists, as it were, on learning the lesson off by heart. This is the minor poet. The minor poet is appreciator rather than creator. He imitates, because he must have his idiom established, acknowledged, labelled in his own consciousness as 'poetic' before he can feel that he is writing poetry. He is always trying to give himself the sensations which he has received from reading the works of greater poets. And since his energies go more into contemplating than creating, it is even possible that he extracts more aesthetic *pleasure* from his own work than the great poet does.

A poetic meaning *is* already in the words and mannerisms which the minor poet is instinctively drawn to use and imitate. Whether it is there as a legacy from the ancient poetic meaning in all language, or whether it is there because it has been put there by some original poet in the past, the fact remains that it is there. It is to do some of my work for me, thinks he (though not, of course, in so many words); let me fit my own emotional experience as neatly as I can into the established poetic moulds, and the result will *give* me something, will comfort *me*, intoxicate *me*.

The great poet, on the contrary, is himself the giver. He is giving out all the time—wisdom to other men, meaning to language. This he does by externalizing as fully as is possible in words his own first-hand experience beyond them. There is, indeed, a certain simplicity and sobriety about the activity of men who expend more energy upon creation than upon appreciation. If they are poets, they do not require to wear their hair long or to neglect their accounts in order to remind themselves of the fact. They are what they are. The difference was well put by Wordsworth:

'The earliest poets of all nations generally wrote from passion excited by real events; they wrote naturally, and as men: feeling powerfully as they did, their language was daring, and figurative. In succeeding times, Poets, and Men ambitious of the fame of Poets, perceiving the influence of such language, and desirous of producing the same effect without being animated by the same passion, set themselves to a mechanical adoption of these figures of speech, and made use of them, sometimes with propriety, but much more frequently applied them to feelings and thoughts with which they had no natural connection whatsoever. A language was thus insensibly produced, differing materially from the real language of men in *any situation*. The Reader or Hearer of this distorted language found himself in a perturbed and unusual state of mind also: in both cases he was willing that his common judgement and understanding should be laid asleep, and he had no instinctive and infallible perception of the true to make him reject the false; the one served as a passport for the other. The emotion was in both cases delightful, and no wonder if he confounded one with the other, and believed them both to be produced by the same, or similar causes. Besides, the Poet spoke to him in the character of a man to be looked up to, a man of genius and authority. Thus, and from a variety of other causes, this distorted language was received with admiration; and Poets, it is probable, who had before contented themselves for the most part with misapplying only expressions which at first had been distorted by real passion, carried the abuse still further, and introduced phrases composed apparently in the spirit of the original figurative language of passion, yet altogether of their own invention, and characterized by various degrees of wanton deviation from good sense and Nature.'[1]

It is just this conservatism, or mimicry, masquerading as archaism, that Wordsworth meant, when *he* used the phrase 'poetic diction'; for at the time when he wrote, it was particularly rampant throughout literature. To him, one mark of the artificiality of this so-called 'poetic diction' was the fact that it had become identified with that artificial opposition between 'poetry' and 'prose' which has already been discovered here. No one would have dreamed of employing the stale Miltonics, which lay at the bottom of so much eighteenth-century 'poetic diction', in *prose*, however imaginative; and Wordsworth, in his *Prefaces*, sought to abolish alike the sham contradiction (poetry *or* prose) and the sham distinction of style on which it was based. To him, as to Sidney, verse was 'but an ornament, and no cause to poetry'.

[1] Appendix on the phrase '*Poetic Diction*'.

Now it is indeed, as Wordsworth pointed out, a fairly sound *negative* test of the poetic value of *verse* to ask oneself whether the same expressions could have been used with propriety in *prose*—provided that one remembers, as he sometimes failed to do, that *the order in which words are placed has become in English an integral part of their meaning.* The test is, therefore, not simply whether the same words could have been used, but whether the same words could have been used in the same order. Since Wordsworth's acute analysis of the causes of bad poetry, the phrase 'poetic diction' has tended to retain its disparaging flavour; and it was principally for this reason that I included the words 'obviously intended to arouse' in the definition which I gave on the first page of this book.

But soon after such a false 'poetic diction' has become established as a fashion, it begins for that reason to destroy itself. The very word 'fashion' implies change; and the absence of change and movement which, as we have seen, are indispensable to the pleasure of appreciation, now makes itself felt, just as it did (II, 3) when I read too many ballads at a sitting. So it comes about (unless there be a grievous dearth of greater poets) that real inspiration, the expression of first-hand spiritual experience, breaks through the shell of poetic posturings embodied in the fashionable diction of the moment, and there is a 'Return to Nature'. An American writer has remarked of the period between Milton and Wordsworth that it 'ended in a wholesale abolishment of "Poetic Diction", and a return to the spoken language'. And then she adds: 'We do not usually recall that it began in exactly the same manner'.[1]

[1] M. L. Barstow: Wordsworth's *Theory of Poetic Diction*, p. 24.

There is little doubt that nearly every poetic *fashion* (to use a word more in keeping with the trivial nature of the thing) begins in this way as a return to Nature, or in other words a return to the attempted expression of genuine knowledge. And this return to Nature itself, this breaking through the shell of the *old* poetic fashion, which is clearly the very opposite of conservatism, may yet be very closely allied to archaism. True archaism does imply, not a standing still, but a *return* to something older, and if we examine it more closely, we shall find that it generally means a movement towards language at an earlier stage of its own development. Nothing further, it is hoped, need be said as to the general reasons why language at an earlier stage of its own development should be more suitable for poetic expression, or why a return in that direction should correspond in some degree with a return to 'Nature'. That the two do in fact often go together is palpable from the history of European literature.

[4]

Archaism, whether grammatical or selective, takes in the main two different forms, which I will call here the literary and the colloquial. Literary archaism resuscitates out of academic knowledge words and forms which have actually fallen out of use altogether. So Spenser, in order to express a spirit of fantastic chivalry and devotion, which is itself the Middle Ages *as seen from the standpoint of a later consciousness*, found it natural to employ a diction, partly antique and partly invented by himself, of which the main characteristics, however, were undoubtedly drawn from the English language as it had been spoken centuries before his time. So also Dryden, as Gray pointed out in one of his letters, excavated from oblivion many ancient words. And incidentally, since today many of these (for the very reason, presumably, that he resuscitated them) no longer possess an archaic flavour, it is interesting to try and resurrect for ourselves, when reading Dryden, the precise effect with which they must have fallen on the ears of his contemporaries.[1] Lastly, the Romantic Revival, with its double passion for minute observation of nature and for grubbing up medieval words—words whose meanings had never been through the eighteenth-century mill of abstraction—is the most obvious example of all of this literary archaism.

Beside it must be set the colloquial archaism which employs words and forms in spoken, but not in literary use during its own day. The writer of prose, whose material is prosaic, need never diverge very far from the spoken language; and it has been well pointed out that the habit of good conversation probably had something to do with the growth of that lucid and simple prose style which was the crowning literary glory of the eighteenth century. But since poets, unlike prose-writers, learn more from other poets, and are conservative when they are not great, they are apt to lose touch with the language *spoken* by their fellow-men. This language, especially among the simple and unsophisticated part of a population, which is kept

[1] *Array, boon, furbished, crones, wayward, smouldering* are among the many examples which Gray gives in a letter to R. West (1742). The *New English Dictionary*, however, has quotations for most of them between Shakespeare and Dryden.

'close to Nature' by the very necessities of livelihood, is usually representative in some degree of the literary language itself at an earlier stage, and before its meanings had been through that abstracting process which is both cause and effect of the increased intellectual refinement that now differentiates it from 'vulgar speech'. Where that is not so and the vulgar locutions to which a poet flies for life have a late origin—as, for example, in the case of some slang phrases—it is still not wholly unreasonable to use the word 'archaism', since this part of the language is clearly *younger* than the other, that is to say, it is nearer to its own source. For properly understood, archaism chooses, not old words, but young ones. If it is objected that the meaning of *archaism* is here stretched too far, the reply, of course, is that it is only by such deliberate extensions that hitherto unapprehended, or unemphasized, relationships can become incarnate in meaning.

Of such a nature was the colloquial archaism of Dante and indeed of all those European poets who first abandoned Latin for their native tongues. Just as it was conservatism which retained Latin for so long as the literary language of Europe, so we may call it archaism which at last saw and welcomed the poetic value, the freshness, the touch of Nature, without which there can be no true wisdom, in the young idiom of Romance and the barbarous dissonance of the Northern races.

In France, Ronsard and Du Bellay seem to have combined both kinds of archaism, while Malherbe in the seventeenth century pressed the colloquial variety with such good will that he well-nigh abolished for his native country the whole distinction between a prosaic language and a language of poetry.[1] Consequently, during the eighteenth century, it was difficult for a French writer to be either *very* poetic or very prosaic. The best French verse represents an essentially prosaic idiom carried as near the poetic as it will go. It tends to be of the kind depicted in VII, 6, in which the poet actually assists, instead of opposing, the normal 'progress' of language. But in English literature, while all the great poets have instinctively employed more or less of this colloquial archaism, there was nothing of that deliberate and systematic nature which distinguishes Italian and French literary history, until the time of Wordsworth.[2]

These great movements of archaism, which are at the same time returns to Nature, are only inaugurated, as we should expect, by the greater poets. They are led by poets with something to say, in other words, with something to give. It is these who break away from the old 'poetic diction' in its futile sense, and it is not their fault that what they create eventually becomes a new one. At first, indeed, so far from being the fashion, their language is likely to find it difficult to get a hearing at all. For the critic, like the

[1] Compare the quotation from Gray's letter in section I of this chapter. 'Cette simplicité presque banale des termes employés lui [Malherbe] faisait dire que les crocheteurs du Port au Foin étaient ses maîtres en fait de langage.' Petit de Julleville, quoted M. L. Barstow (*v. supra*).

It is significant of the state at which the literary language had arrived in England at about the same time (i.e. before the particular 'return to Nature' which culminated in the diction of Pope and his followers) that the Royal Society itself should have turned for clarity to the language of 'artisans, countrymen, and merchants'. The fact suggests, moreover, that the now somewhat rapidly growing divergence between the meanings of the two words *science* and *knowledge* ought not to be laid to the charge of the original and poetic founders of that institution.

[2] In our own day we have been witnessing the success over a smaller area of the dramatist, J. M. Synge.

minor poet (they are often one even in corporeal substance) needs to have his poetry in an idiom already duly established as poetry, before he can appreciate it as such. And usually nothing but time can bring this about; as the new style percolates through the more lively and original spirits till at last it receives the franchise of the pedants and the literary snobs. Thus, it so often comes about that the fame of great poets is posthumous only. They have, as Shelley said, to create the taste by which they are appreciated; and by the time they have done so, the choice of words, the new meaning and manner of speech which they have brought in *must*, by the nature of things, be itself growing heavier and heavier, hanging like a millstone of authority round the neck of free expression. We have but to substitute dogma for literature, and we find the same endless antagonism between prophet and priest. How shall the hard rind not hate and detest the unembodied life that is cracking it from within? How shall the mother not feel pain?

XI

STRANGENESS

[1]

The question has often been raised whether or no poets make good critics. Is it an advantage, it is asked, that the critic should himself be creative? Those who hold that it is not, point out that the powerful imagination of a poet may easily by stimulated by some experience of which the artistic ingredients are in themselves trivial, or non-existent, so that the poet-critic may mistake his own poetic contribution for that of the original author. 'Tipperary' on a barrel organ may move him more than the Ninth Symphony; let him beware, therefore, of expressing an opinion of music. On the other hand, really dreadful pitfalls open at the feet of the unpoetic critic. For, since his principal function is appreciation, it follows that the prosaic —the death-forces—are particularly strong in him. Therefore, if his endless appraisals are not leavened by some creative vigour of his own, he is in danger of losing all sympathy with the Poetic itself, that bodiless ocean of life out of which all works of art spring. Nay, he may even cease to believe in it. For the pure prosaic can apprehend nothing but *results*. It knows nought of the thing coming into being, only of the thing become. It cannot realize *shapes*. It sees nature—and would like to see art—as a series of mechanical rearrangements of *facts*. And facts are *facta*—things done and past.

Consequently the non-creative critic can never be the interpreter proper (VIII, 4); he can only be the *collector*. As time passes and the dammed springs of poetic impulse which first impelled him to criticism dry up, his criticism becomes no more than a hunting for subtle sensations and high flavours, and then a nice classification of these according to similar sensations and flavours enjoyed in the past. He invents proper epithets like *Dantesque*, *Dickensian*, *Shavian*, to save himself the trouble of interpretation; and these become less and less significant as they are drawn from more and more minor artists; till at last his work tells us nothing about its subject-matter and too much about its author.

It may, however, be asked why an interpreter should be necessary or desirable. The answer to this lies in the nature of inspiration. And it should be apparent that, the more perfectly balanced are the two principles in the poet himself, the more control he has of his inspiration, the less necessary an interpreter becomes. The perfect poet would express himself perfectly. It is for those writers in whom the rational is too weak for the poetic, whose critical consciousness is dimmed therefore by their inspiration, that we need an interpreter. Such writers may be compared to the seers that most communities revere before they have reached the period of balance between the two principles, and while their poetic—unindividualized—still predominates. Thus, Plato points out in the *Timaeus* that the seers need 'prophetae' to interpret their meaning. 'For no one', he says, 'attains to true and inspired consciousness while in full possession of his wits, but either the power of his intellect is restricted in sleep, or it is changed by some disease or divine possession.' And he adds that the task of *remembering* the vision, whether it be a waking or a sleeping one, and of understanding it, is reserved for reason and the full consciousness. The seer himself, on the other hand, while he is still 'raving' and remains *in* the inspiration, cannot judge of his own vision and words.

This inability to judge and to express himself, however, is not a virtue in a modern poet. Poetry, in our time, implies *expression*, and therefore judgement. For us, the perfect poet is also the perfect critic. There remains nevertheless the critical interpretation of imperfect poetry; there is still plenty of work for the genuine critic. A controlled and fundamentally sane consciousness, a gentle sympathetic imaginative understanding, not only of 'human nature' in the ordinary sense, but of the nature of inspiration and of its function in human evolution—these are the proper equipment of the serious critic; these are the first weapons he must use in his difficult task of distinguishing the true poetic from the merely aesthetic—or, in looser speech, great poetry from poetry. And in doing so he will be confronted with the problem of *strangeness*.

[2]

A few further remarks are required on the fact, noted at the beginning of this book, that almost any kind of 'strangeness' may produce an aesthetic effect, that is to say, an effect which, however slight, is qualitatively the same as that of serious poetry. On examination, the sole condition is found to be this, that the strangeness shall have an *interior* significance; it must be felt as arising from a different plane or mode of consciousness, and not merely as eccentricity of expression. It must be a strangeness of *meaning*. Thus, if I invent the meaningless word, *hexterabonto*, and insert it in a line of verse, it can add nothing (outside of its sound value) to the aesthetic effect.

Moreover, this outlandishness is, as we have seen, the part of poetry with which the actual *pleasure* of appreciation—the old, authentic thrill, which is so strong that it binds some men to their libraries for a lifetime, and actually hinders them from increasing knowledge—is most closely connected. This is that 'element of strangeness in all beauty' which has been remarked in one way or another by so many critics. Alike in the greatest poetry and in the least, if pleasure is to arise, it must be there. And conversely, where it is, there will be some aesthetic pleasure. Thus, in Example I we saw how even the laughable semantic struggles of Pidgin English have their aesthetic value; nor is this simpler kind of strangeness by any means only to be found in the Southern Hemisphere. Aristotle in his *Poetics* showed that he knew the aesthetic value of 'unfamiliar words',[1] among which he included 'foreign expressions'[2]; in keeping diction above the 'ordinary'[3] level; and anyone who has been to the trouble of learning a foreign language after the age at which he had reached a certain degree of aesthetic maturity, will know that aesthetic pleasure arises

[1] γλῶτται. [2] ξενικοί λόγοι. [3] ἰδιωτικόν.

from the contemplation of quite ordinary expressions couched in a foreign idiom. It is important, then, to note that this is not, in so far as it is aesthetic, the pleasure of comparing different ways of saying the same thing, but the pleasure of realizing the *slightly different thing that is said.* For, outside the purest abstractions and technicalities, no two languages can ever say quite the same thing.

[3]

A certain foreign element, impinging on the native genius, has, in point of fact, played a fairly prominent part in the history of English poetry. Who can say how much of the delicious freshness and perfume that hangs about Chaucer's loveliest lines is due to the presence of all those French words, many of them employed in English for the first time in the passage we are reading, and nearly all of them comparatively new to the language? And if no other English poet had the same magnificent opportunity of actually borrowing strange words, yet, over and over again, the foreign element has been strong enough to make itself felt idiomatically against a background formed by the genius of our own language. Gray in a letter to Wharton[1] actually distinguishes two French and three Italian 'schools' between his own day and Chaucer's; and it is significant that (especially up to the Elizabethan period) so much of our poetry should have consisted of translations from the French, which are not infrequently better than their originals!

[1] April 15, 1770.

[4]

There are many other examples of this semi-accidental kind of strangeness, among which might be placed various words accepted for centuries past—not apparently because they are older, nor indeed for any discernible reason—as *poetic* in contradistinction to a parallel *prosaic* word for almost the same thing. *Slumber*, *bale*, *dire*, *billow* occur readily to the mind, and there are numberless other examples. Often we find that such words have also continued to survive in dialect use. One wonders, therefore, if their poetic *imprimatur* may not in some cases have been given them by purely accidental circumstances. The tacit agreement to 'drop' a certain word is a well-known phenomenon in the history of language, especially where there happens to be another word practically synonymous with it. Thus, at a time when such a word as *slumber* had first been dropped from ordinary conversational use, its appearance in a ballad or the work of some local poet would no doubt have aroused the pleasure of strangeness in other poets, and so have tempted them to continue making use of it themselves.

[5]

More deliberate, and of a much later date, is the introduction of a certain class of word which I shall describe imperfectly as *technical*. This was an effect of which the Metaphysicals were particularly fond, and there is an undeniable touch of magic in it. Thus, when George Herbert speaks of bringing his heart to the Lord in a *dish of fruit*, or describes how

> *When God at first made man,*
> *Having a* glass *of blessings standing by,*
> *'Let us', said He, 'pour on him all we can; . . .'*

the appearance in such surroundings of these plain, cold, manufactured articles imports an atmosphere of wizardry that is both peculiar and moving. Herbert often sought to secure this effect even in the titles of his poems, *The Collar*, *The Pulley*, *The Bag*, etc., being all names of lyrics whose real, immediate subject is the relation of God and man. Wordsworth produces a similar atmosphere in the following beautiful quatrain from *The Reverie of Poor Susan*:

> *'Tis a note of enchantment; what ails her? She sees*
> *A mountain ascending, a vision of trees;*
> *Bright volumes of vapour through Lothbury glide,*
> *And a river flows on through the vale of Cheapside.*

And in our own day Mr. G. K. Chesterton, both in prose and verse, is a past master of this particular effect, which might be described as the art of concentrating attention on a familiar thing by making it stand out suddenly from an unfamiliar background.

This device affects the soul in a manner which is perhaps most adequately expressed by the French verb *frapper*. A similar effect is obtained by slightly different means in the use of words which are *technical* in the stricter sense, as being part of the jargon of a special art or trade. Malherbe, who said that he used the language of 'crocheteurs', qualified his statement by adding 'only so far as it is generally intelligible'; but Dryden, scorning such a negative system of selection, boasted that he was 'not ashamed to *learn* something about language from sailors'. Nor was navigation the only trade whose vocabulary appealed to him in this way; few people today would deny the fine effect of the lines from *St. Cecilia's Day*:

From harmony, from heavenly harmony,
This universal frame began:
From harmony to harmony
Through all the compass of the notes it ran,
The diapason closing full in Man.

Johnson, however, censured Dryden for the use of such a technical term as *diapason* on the ground that 'all appropriated terms of art should be sunk in general expressions, because poetry is to speak a general language'.

Here we must gently but firmly insist that Johnson was hopelessly wrong—unless by 'general' he merely meant 'intelligible'. For if there is anything besides their strangeness which might commend these technical words to a poet, it would be just the fact that they are *not* general. They express, as nearly as any word can do, a concrete, particular *thing*, and not an abstract, generalized *idea*. The theory of this has already been partly discussed and will be developed farther in an Appendix; but it may be worth pointing out here an instinctive tendency in poets, and others, to use *general* terms of things which they are ignorant of or despise, or in which they can discern no poetic value, and *particular*—even technical—terms of things which really inspire them. Love is the begetter of intimate knowledge; for what we love it is not tedious, but delightful, to observe minutely.[1] Wordsworth's 'itinerant vehicle' has already been quoted: one thinks of what Dickens could make, alike of that same conveyance and of the dinner-table which to Wordsworth is only the 'social board'. Pope, on the other hand, will generalize the meadows which Wordsworth never tires of describing in lovingest detail, under some such phrase as 'flowery mead', while the contents of Belinda's toilet-table receive from his pen their proper names.

All this, however, is somewhat of a digression, since the point here is not the value of appropriate or technical words in their own sphere, but their effectiveness when carried outside it. It is the outsider, not the *habitué*, who appreciates the poetic value of the technical terms and peculiar idiom of a science, an art, or a trade—a value, be it said, which is often exceedingly high. No genuine lover of poetry and of words can pick up a book on, say, Botany or Metallurgy, and read of *spores* and *capsules* and *lanceolate* leaves, of *pearly* and *adamantine lustres*, without feeling poetically enriched by that section of the new vocabulary which actually impinges on his own present consciousness of Nature. Nor can he even listen to a circle of enthusiasts—sailors, golfers, wireless men, actors, and the like—riding, as they do, their special hobby-horses idiomatically over all departments of life, without being delighted, without being *frappé* (for a short time only) by the result.

[1] Hatred, as in the case of satire, or any powerful feeling, may lead to a similar result. It is really indifference, alone, which accepts generalization as sufficient.

[6]

At the risk of tedious repetition, I would insist once more that this aesthetic value of strangeness overlaps, but does not coincide with, the ancient and proverbial truism that familiarity breeds contempt. It is not correlative with wonder; for wonder is our reaction to things which we are conscious of not quite understanding, or at any rate of understanding less than we had thought. The element of strangeness in beauty has the contrary effect. It arises from contact with a different kind of *consciousness* from our own, different, yet not so remote that we cannot partly share it, as indeed, in such a connection, the mere word 'contact' implies. Strangeness, in fact, arouses wonder when we do not understand; aesthetic imagination when we do.

XII

CONCLUSION

[1]

The various instances of strangeness which have just been cited were of a somewhat accidental and trivial nature. But there is, as we have seen, one kind which is not accidental at all, and which, irrespective of these others, can always be produced where a creative imagination is wedded to an acute intellect. In very strict speech I think it should be distinguished, as the truly *poetic*, from the other, merely *aesthetic*, varieties of strangeness. This kind depends, not so much upon the difference between two kinds of consciousness or outlook, as on the act of becoming conscious itself. It is the momentary apprehension of the poetic by the rational, into which the former is for ever transmuting itself—which it is itself for ever in process of becoming. This is what I would call pure poetry. This is the very moonlight of our experience, true and ever-recurring begetter of strangeness; it is the pure idea of strangeness, to which all the others are but imperfect approximations, tainted with personal accidents. It is this which gives to great poetry its 'inevitability', distinguishing it from the thousands of delicious trifles that are commonly allowed to be poetic without being great—trifles which, in precise moments, *I* would only allow to be 'aesthetic'. And since Mind existed, as Life, and Meaning, before it become conscious of itself, as knowledge, not only the activity of great poets, but mere lapse of time may sometimes be a sufficient cause of this archetypal strangeness.

[2]

The Meaning of life is continually being dried up, as it were, and left for dead in the human mind by the operation of a purely discursive intellectual activity, of which language—builded, as it is, on the impact of sense perceptions—is the necessary tool. This discursive activity is inseparable from human *self*-consciousness, out of which it would kill, alike the given Meanings of which language, at its early stages, still retains an echo, and the meanings which individual poets have inserted into it later by their creative activity in metaphor. 'Language', wrote Emerson, in a flash of insight which covers practically all that has been written in these pages, 'is fossil poetry.'

Living poetry, on the other hand—the present stir of aesthetic imagination—lights up only when the normal continuum of this process is interrupted in such a manner that a kind of gap is created, and an earlier impinges directly upon a later—a more living upon a more conscious. This is the justification of archaism; and to a consideration of the more technical kind of archaism, such as was attempted above, a poetic history of language would have to add some account of the part played in, for instance, English literature by revivals of older modes of consciousness as a whole. It would approach from this point of view the Renaissance and the Romantic Revival, and again, the work of individual poets, such as Keats, whose poetic character is almost inseparable from the impact on his modern imagination of the ancient world of Greek myth. It might well go on to consider the re-emergence at intervals of certain particular streams of living meaning, such as that contained in Greek myth itself—Platonism—Esoteric Christianity; and the way in which poetry has blossomed afresh and in different places, every time they have broken through.

[3]

The many critics—among them Johnson and Coleridge—who have insisted that the principal object of poetry is to arouse *pleasure*, were no doubt partly goaded into this opinion by their reaction against a superficially didactic view. But there remains nevertheless a deep truth in their contention. If not the prime *object*, pleasure is undoubtedly an excellent test, or mark,[1] of the presence of poetry. For what is absolutely necessary to the present existence of poetry? Movement. The wisdom which she has imparted may remain for a time at rest, but she herself will always be found to have gone forward to where there is life, and therefore movement, *now*. And we have seen that the experience of aesthetic pleasure betrays the real presence of movement, even though its cause be accidental, even though we ourselves have brought about the conditions for it by pretending to forget what we are and know.

But without the continued existence of poetry, without

[1] See page 41.

a steady influx of new meaning into language, even the knowledge and wisdom which poetry herself has given in the past must wither away into a species of mechanical calculation. Great poetry is the progressive incarnation of life in consciousness. Hence the absolute value of aesthetic pleasure as a criterion; for before we can feel it, we must have become aware in some degree of the actual progress—not merely of its results. Over the perpetual evolution of human consciousness, which is stamping itself upon the transformation of language, the spirit of poetry hovers, for ever unable to alight. It is only when we are lifted above that transformation, so that we behold it as present movement, that our startled souls feel the little pat and the throbbing, feathery warmth, which tell us that she has perched. It is only when we have risen from beholding the creature into beholding creation that our mortality catches for a moment the music of the turning spheres.

APPENDIX I

NOTE ON CHAPTER II

I have not felt called upon to prescribe the exact extent to which the expression 'felt change of consciousness' applies to other arts, though I certainly believe it has meaning for them all. Poetry differs from all her sisters in this one important respect, that (excluding the sound values) consciousness is also the actual *material* in which she works. Consciousness is to her what their various mediums (marble, pigments, etc.) are to the other arts; for words themselves are but τῶν ἐν τῇ ψυχῇ παθημάτων σύμβολα—symbols of consciousness.

As to the so-called 'appreciation' of Nature, the term is, strictly speaking, a misnomer. Nature is only 'appreciated' in this way by reflection from the arts, as is indeed suggested by the application to natural beauty of art words like *romantic*, *scenery*, *picturesque*, etc. We admire not what *we* see but what Corot or Turner, or the illustrator of our favourite fairy-stories, saw in the landscape. But *direct* aesthetic delight in nature comes from our own unaided expansion of our own consciousness in intuition: it is as though we were reading a poem which we ourselves had just written.

APPENDIX II

[1]

It may very well be objected that certain words, as *abstract*, *concrete*, *subjective*, etc., have been used in this book, either in a question-begging manner, or at least without a sufficiently clear indication of what is meant by them. Therefore, while I believe that their significance ought to have emerged gradually from the text itself—provided that it be allowed to stand as a whole—I should like, in the remaining Appendices, to try and state in a somewhat more condensed manner what I intended to convey by these ambiguous symbols.

In explanation of the form of this particular Appendix (II), I might perhaps add that, in the case of *abstract* and *concrete*, it seemed to me that the best way to set their meaning in a clear light was to try and relate what I have said here on the nature of consciousness with some well-known intellectual system. With this end, I took Locke's *Essay on the Human Understanding* and Kant's *Critique of Pure Reason* and endeavoured to locate their precise point of departure from my own premises and conclusions. I chose Locke, partly because he paid such particular attention to language, partly because he is English, and partly because it seems to me that historically the Essay does really mark a very important initial step in the development of those intellectual premises (they are premises *now*) which make it so difficult for Western thought to grasp the true nature of inspiration. So far I have only hinted at these premises under cover of such words as *abstraction* (as used in the loose sense) or '*logomorphism*'.

Kant, on the other hand, I selected because, with all his contempt of Locke, it seems to me that the *Critique of Pure Reason* was one of the most effective intellectual factors in finally clenching these premises upon the minds of almost the whole Western world. It is not merely a matter of acknowledged supremacy, though he is indeed revered by many as the Aristotle of post-Christian thought; I follow Steiner (to whose *Philosophie der Freiheit*[1] and *Wahrheit und Wissenschaft*[1] I am here very much indebted) in detecting an unacknowledged influence far wider still. How many children, I wonder, are nowadays informed at an early age by some elder brother or some guide, philosopher, and friend, that what they see and hear and smell is not 'nature' but the activity of their own nerves? And though this is not Kant's doctrine, it *is* a crude physiological reflection of it. Thus, it does not require a very active fancy to see the Königsberg ghost hovering above, and intertwining itself with the ideas of minds that never even knew Kant's name; and this indirect influence may be just as strong over others which are also directly acquainted with his books—and perhaps even despise them. In Croce's honest words, Kantian doctrine is '(so to say) immanent in all modern thought'.

[1] Translated into English, and published in one volume under the title *The Philosophy of Spiritual Activity*.

[2]

The word *abstract*, as applied to thoughts or to the meanings of words, should not be very hard to define; for there is nothing abhorrent in it from the nature of definition itself. Indeed, it is fairly correct to say that the meaning of a word is abstract, just in so far as it is definable. The definition of a word, which we find in a Dictionary—inasmuch as it is not conveyed by synonym and metaphor, or illustrated by quotation—*is* its most abstract meaning. And if, when using the word in thought or speech, we are prepared, as Pascal suggested in his *Esprit Géométrique*, to substitute for the word itself its definition, 'denuding it of all additional meaning', then we are thinking or speaking abstractly. Thus, in thinking of *gold*, if we can at any point in our thought substitute 'a precious, yellow, non-rusting, malleable, ductile metal of high specific gravity', then our thought of gold is relatively abstract. A purely abstract term—which, with the possible exception of numbers,[1] can nowhere exist—is a mark representing, not a thing or being, but the fact *that* identical sensations *have been* experienced on two or more occasions. It is in fact a *classification* of sense-perceptions. Purely abstract thinking, carried to its logical conclusions, is thus—counting;[1] as was realized by Hobbes, who described all thinking as addition and subtraction, and by Leibnitz who, regarding perception itself as a kind of imperfect thought, described it as 'unconscious numeration'.

[1] The Arabic system of numeration, of which practically the entire meaning resides in the *order* in which the figures are arranged, furnishes an interesting commentary on the parallel progress of language towards increased fixity of word-order and abstraction of content. V, 3, etc.

Now the meaning of nearly every word, as was pointed out in III, 2, can *apparently* be interpreted, on an etymological analysis, in terms of pure sense-perceptions. Let us say, then, that every word, in so far as it is interpreted to 'mean' the percept itself, is *material*; in so far as it is interpreted to mean the fact of the repetition of percepts, is *abstract*; in so far as it is interpreted to mean the percepts plus the real but imperceptible link between them, is *concrete*. It could be shown without much difficulty that the first interpretation is simply the fruit of confused thinking, while the second is possible, but is equivalent to numeration.

Where the denotation of the word seems at first sight to be wholly remote from the physical world, as in the case of *virtue*, we shall still find that, in so far as we consider it to be susceptible of scientific 'definition'—in so far, that is, as its meaning is *abstract* to us—it is ultimately reducible to terms of sensation plus numeration. Thus, even if we call virtue an 'impulse' to perform certain actions, we are left with the obligation to define impulse; nor will it be long before we are talking about 'pushing'. But what can a push be but a 'force', i.e. a something, an *x*, an abstraction definable only by its observed numerical effects? And even if we give up this attempt at pure definition (= pure abstraction) and, taking just a *little* help from metaphor, affirm the existence of a 'moral world' imperceptible to the senses, we are still quite incapable of *defining* virtue, except by its observed effects. A far bolder activity of the imagination is necessary before the concept 'virtue', in its radiant and practical reality, can be lit up in one mind by suggestion from another. And the same is true of gold.

An excellent example of language at an advanced stage of abstraction is the English language, as Locke sought to interpet it. His definitions of words are perfect models of abstract thought, and he proceeded to attribute this defining activity of his own to primitive man, as the process by which language actually came into being.

'One of Adam's children [he wrote], roving in the mountains, lights on a glittering substance which pleases his eye. Home he carries it to Adam, who, upon consideration of it, finds it to be hard, to have a bright yellow colour, and an exceeding great weight. There, perhaps, at first, are all the qualities he takes notice of in it; and abstracting this complex idea, consisting of a substance having that peculiar bright yellowness, and a weight very great in proportion to its bulk, he gives the name *zahab*, to denominate and mark all substances that have these sensible qualities in them.'[1]

This is the kind of thing I mean by 'logomorphism' as an *historical* delusion. It can also, as will be seen later, be a psychological delusion.

[3]

Just as a concrete definition is an impossibility, so it is much harder to give even an approximate definition of the word *concrete* itself—not, of course, of the simple, physical meaning commonly attached to it in Logic primers, but in the sense in which it has been used in this book. It is difficult, because one is brought face to face, on the very threshold, with the whole mystery of creation—and even

[1] *Essay on the Human Understanding*, III, vi, 46.

incarnation; with the mystery, in fact, of Meaning itself and of the qualitative reality which definition automatically excludes. If I were to bring the reader into my presence and point to an actual lump of gold, without even opening my mouth and uttering the word *gold*—then, this much at least could be said, that he would have had from me nothing that was *not* concrete. But that does not take us very far. For it does not follow that he would possess anything but the most paltry and inchoate knowledge of the whole reality—'gold'. The depth of such knowledge would depend entirely on how many he might by his own activity have intuited of the innumerable concepts, which are as much a part of the reality as the percepts or sense-data,[1] and some of which he must already have made his own before he could even observe what I am pointing to as an 'object' at all (cf. II, 5). Other concepts—already partially abstracted when I name them—such as the gleaming, the hardness to the touch, the resemblance to the light of the sun, its part in human history, as well as those contained in the dictionary definition—all these may well comprise a little, but still only a very little, more of the whole meaning.

Both in the text and here, therefore, it has not been possible to do much more than hint at the nature of concrete meaning and the knowledge of it. Nor am I unaware of the unsatisfactory nature of the particular hint which I

[1] Really very much so, since the perceptual part of his experience is conditioned by his own physical organization, his position in space in relation to the object, etc., etc. Thus, in so far as it is perceptual only, his experience, though always concrete, is subjectively determined: and his *knowledge* of the reality will vary directly as the extent to which he can disentangle these determinations from it, by knowing them too.

attempted to give in IV, 1, of some conceivably more *concrete* inflexion of the verb 'to cut'. For apart from the word 'I', the phrase 'I cut this flesh with joy' represents, as it stands, merely an addition to the abstract 'cut' of other more or less abstract ideas. It must, however, be remembered that it is just a part of the point at issue that reality is *not* susceptible of direct expression in modern language. Thus, the meaning of the whole passage is accessible only to the active imagination of the reader himself, if he has good will enough to try and reconstruct for himself, on the basis of what is given, the consciousness of the hypothetical individual who heard or uttered the hypothetical word.

[4]

Following from the above, we shall find it particularly important to realize that the operation in the poet of the unitary principle which I characterized as 'poetic' by no means coincides with the 'synthesis' of modern philosophy and psychology. The latter word is generally used, whether deliberately or no, in the sense of a synthesis of *ideas* already abstract. The former, on the other hand, is always a direct conceptual linking of percept to percept, or image to image, from the bottom of the scale upwards (II, 5), and is therefore justly labelled *aesthetic*. Though pictorial images in the memory may be substituted for the actual sense-data, it is a peculiar mark of this poetic cognition (*inspiration*) that it commonly has a counter-effect (*recognition*) on the very *observation* through which it has been generated in the first instance. This is much less likely to be the case with opinions or judgements that owe their origin in part to 'synthesis' in the sense in which that word is commonly used. Thus, my experience in observation of apple-blossom is not much affected by my judgement that the tree before me is of the genus *pyrus malus*, which is of the order *Rosaceae*. All this judgement can do for me is to direct me to *look out* for a possible real resemblance between apple-blossom, pear-blossom, and roses, which, as it is intuited in actual observation, becomes poetic knowledge (*inspiration*), and will then react, as wisdom, on my further experience in observation (*recognition*), so that I shall truly see or 'read' the flowers with different eyes.[1]

Now this judgement, even in its present logistic form, could never have been produced by analysis only. Thus, synthesis, as well as analysis, is not a poetic, but a discursive function, operating *within* the sphere of the rational principle. And, for example, Locke's distinction between Wit and Judgement, which might appear at first to be a representation of the two principles traced in this book, is in reality very different.[2] Locke, who started out with 'simple ideas', never discriminated between *percept* and *idea*; he did not see that the idea must already contain a concep-

[1] It is not denied that this judgement itself may have been mediated originally by the poetic principle operating in language and in the minds of botanists and others. The question to be considered is degree of remoteness from the concrete unity. Were plants classified *solely* — as they have been classified by Linnaeus — by the number of their stamens, my judgements derived from the study of botany would probably be altogether useless except for the purpose of logical classification. That is to say, they would be useless, not only aesthetically, but in a most practical way, in that I should not have, e.g., the faintest idea how to produce certain plants from certain soils — just as we have already lost most of our knowledge of the healing properties of herbs.

[2] *Essay on the Human Understanding*, II, xi, 2.

tual element. Hence his synthetic faculty of Wit is synthetic only in the discursive or logistic sense of divining the general in the particular. It conducts a synthesis of *ideas*. Now this is precisely what I understand by the word *definition*. The whole philosophy of Locke might indeed be described as a Philosophy of Definition; hence, no doubt, the amount of space which he devoted to language.

All this is 'synthesis' in exactly the sense in which Aristotle uses the word in the *De Anima*,[1] distinguishing it from knowledge proper and pointing out that it is the beginning of error. It is the beginning of error because it is only the 'putting together' of subjective 'ideas'. And this putting together can only come *after*, and *by means of*, a certain discrimination of actual phenomena—a seeing of them as *separate* sensible objects—without which the ideas themselves (general notions) could never have existed. The poetic principle, on the contrary, was already operative before such discrimination took place, and, when it continues to operate afterwards in inspiration, it operates *in spite of* that discrimination and seeks to undo its work. The poetic conducts *an immediate conceptual synthesis of percepts*. Brought into contact with these by its partial attachment to some individual human brain and body, it meets—through the senses—the *disjecta membra* of a real world, and weaves them again into the one real whole; whence it was called—not perhaps very happily—by Coleridge *esemplastic* (εἰς ἓν πλάττειν).

[1] Bk. III, ch. 6. It is remarkable that the Greeks seem to have had an instinctive horror of the very logic which it was obviously their mission to develop: for Æschylus uses συνθετοὶ λόγοι in the sense of mere 'fiction', which are, he says, 'of all things most hateful to the gods'.

[5]

The same—to take one more example—may be said of Kant's two principles—the Faculty of Distinction and the Faculty of Wit.[1] Both, as he describes them, are discursive. It is true that he postulates an aesthetic 'synthesis' or 'conjunction' as necessarily *preceding* that analytical function of the understanding which makes abstraction possible. But this he calls 'the mere operation of the imagination—a blind but indispensable function of the soul without which we should have no cognition whatever, but of the working of which we are seldom even conscious. . . .' This is, of course, the 'primary' imagination with which Coleridge was so much concerned; but the time of psychology was not yet, and Kant was not interested in it. 'The first thing [he continues] which must be given us in order to the *a priori* cognition of all objects, is the diversity of the pure intuition; the synthesis of this diversity by means of the imagination is the second; but this gives, as yet, no cognition.'[2]

Thus, it is really our necessary *unconsciousness of self* during the actual moment at which this true, aesthetic synthesis, or act of primary imagination, takes place which makes Kant deny to it the name of 'cognition'. He goes on to point out that 'the conceptions which give unity to this pure synthesis, and which consist solely in the representation of this necessary synthetical unity, furnish the third requisite for the cognition of an object, and these conceptions are given by the understanding'.[2]

What are these conceptions, 'which consist solely in the representation of this necessary synthetical unity'?

[1] *Critique of Pure Reason.* Meiklejohn, p. 401. [2] *Ibid.*, pp. 62–63.

Now Kant, in his theory of knowledge, implicitly accepts, as *given*, the subjectivity of the individual.[1] And it is just this fallacy[2] which is at the bottom of what I have called 'Logomorphism'. Kant's thought is thus extremely 'logomorphic', though in a slightly different sense from that in which I first used the word. For he is logomorphic, not historically, but psychologically. He starts his theory of knowledge, not from *thinking*, but from *Kant thinks*. This *Kant thinks*—the 'synthetical unity of apperception'—is to him 'the highest point with which we must connect every operation of the understanding, even the whole of logic and after it our transcendental philosophy: indeed, this faculty is the understanding itself'.

He thus identifies *thinking* with *Kant thinks* and *Kant thinks* with the understanding—which is 'the faculty of judging'. In other words, thinking = judging: 'The same function which gives unity to the different representations in a judgement, gives also unity to the mere synthesis of representations in an intuition.'[3]

The result is the same as that which arose in Locke's case through the confusion of *percept* with *idea*. All cognition is conceived of as being logical in form: and is of the definable only. Kant's answer to the question asked at the end of the last paragraph is, therefore: 'the Categories'. Consequently

[1] It is, however, exceedingly difficult to follow his argument through the tangle of unstable terminology, and at least one passage, wherein he speaks of 'transcendental unity of apperception' and 'objective unity of self-consciousness', seems to admit of an interpretation quite contrary to the main thread of the *Critique*.

[2] See Appendix IV.

[3] It must be remembered that Kant uses *intuition* in a different sense from that in which it is used in this book. For him it corresponds more with *percept* than with *intuition*, as I use the word.

the 'unity' to which he refers is really the unity produced out of a logistic process of *comparison*, that is to say, it is a unity based on the synthesis and analysis of *ideas*—which do indeed posit a remembering, comparing, judging *subject*.[1] In other words, it is the unity of the general notion, the 'nominal essence' of Locke, the 'abstract universal' of V, I; and it has really very little to do with the concrete unity of any complex of percepts which we may have learnt actually to recognize as an 'object'. The only relation it can have to this real unity is the relation of a shadow to a body, whose outer shape the shadow will resemble more or less according to circumstances.[2]

[6]

In his *Essence of Aesthetic* (p. 26) Croce shows that it is because he accepts Kant's theory of cognition that he is

[1] 'All general conceptions—as such—depend for their existence on the analytical unity of consciousness.' (*Ibid.*, p. 82, note.)

[2] There is a curious, somewhat equivocal, passage in the *Critique*, in which Kant himself seems to suggest that the one kind of unity at any rate 'presupposes' the other:

'If the diversity existing in phenomena — a diversity not of form (for in this they may be similar) but of content — were so great that the subtlest human reason could never by comparison discover in them the least similarity (which is not impossible), in this case the logical law of genera would be without foundation, the conception of genus, nay all general conceptions would be impossible, and the faculty of the understanding, the exercise of which is restricted to the world of conceptions, could not exist. The logical principle of genera, accordingly, if it is to be applied to nature (by which I mean objects presented to our senses), presupposes a transcendental principle. In accordance with this principle, homogeneity is necessarily presupposed in the variety of phenomena (although we are unable to determine *a priori* the degree of this homogeneity), because without it no empirical conceptions, and consequently no experience, would be possible.' (*Ibid.*, p. 401).

obliged to divorce art from knowledge altogether. Criticizing the doctrine of an 'esemplastic' imagination, he remarks that 'in any case, the concept or idea always unites the intelligible to the sensible, and not only in art, for the new concept of the concept, first stated by Kant and (so to say) immanent in all modern thought, heals the breach between the sensible and the intelligible worlds, conceives the concept as judgement, and the judgement as synthesis *a priori*, and the synthesis *a priori* as the word becoming flesh, as history. Thus that definition of art leads imagination back to logic and art to philosophy, contrary to intention.'

Croce thus follows Kant in just this all-important point of identifying thinking with judging. Therefore he dislikes the notion that imagination is 'esemplastic', is related in any way to thinking and knowing.

For we see from the first few words quoted that, just as Locke identified *percept* with *idea*, so the Kantian identifies *idea* with *concept*. Whereas the idea is, in truth—as Steiner has so well pointed out—a *result* which the concept brings about in uniting itself to the percept. It stands between percept and concept, and is the beginning of subjectivity. If the idea is thought, the concept is thinking.

I pause here for emphasis. The distinction is absolutely crucial. If thinking is really identical with judging, instead of merely including it—then Croce's aesthetic *may* be quite sound—but I *must* be talking nonsense.

It is perhaps hardly necessary to add that 'Realism', in the sense of an hypostatization of such *ideas*, must be merely one step further into the realm of unreality. For it is a step into the realm of shadows of shadows. Such hypostatization is today commonly attributed to, e.g., Plato, and that not only by amateurs in philosophy, but even by those who have made it their principal task to interpret him to others, and who, following Kant, regard it as a matter of course that they know what the author of *Timaeus* meant better than he did himself. Thus, it may be remarked, in conclusion, that logomorphism is always to be suspected in the writing of modern commentators, etc., upon ancient philosophy or literature. It is precisely when such a writer starts complaining that his author uses the same word in two different senses that the discerning reader will prick up the ears of his imagination in the hope of acquiring some real knowledge. 'Equivocation', or 'amphibology', as they sometimes call it, should never be imputed, until we have thoroughly satisfied ourselves that the two ideas, which the author in question is accused of confusing, had a separate existence in his time comparable to that which they have in our own. So ubiquitous is the Königsberg ghost that it is, in my opinion, wise to assume every modern writer on every subject to be guilty of logomorphism, until he has actually produced some evidence of his innocence.

APPENDIX III

SEE CHAPTER IV, 3

[1]

It is by no means suggested that the two kinds of metaphor—true and accidental—are easy to distinguish, or that any infallible criterion can be supplied. No doubt both may co-exist in a single phrase. Nevertheless, I believe that discrimination on purely aesthetic grounds, may be buttressed and steadied by a wise and imaginative understanding of the historical progress of language and consciousness, and that has been my excuse for writing this book. Since I have already devoted considerable space to expounding the nature of what I call *true* metaphor and simile, I will only add here a very few words on the false, or accidental, kind. Firstly, it must be understood that this kind of metaphor, properly employed, may be (i) useful, (ii) delightful, and (iii) influential in the evolution of language.

It is useful, for example, in the exposition of an argument, and in the calling up of clear visual images, as when I ask you to think of the earth as a great orange with a knitting needle stuck through it—or call the sky an inverted bowl—two images in which there can at least be no more than a minimum of poetic truth. It is delightful, alike as cause of strangeness (Chap. IX), as a kind of irresponsible juggling with the universe *in abstracto* (the Elizabethan 'conceit', the *Witch of Atlas*, etc.) and as the vehicle of passion, which has been forced to an exceptionally high point of intensity without transcending the limits of the personal—so that we experience the poetic energy in the form of heat or pressure rather than in that of light:

Fall, winter, fall; for he,
Prompt hand and headpiece clever,
Has woven a winter robe,
And made of earth and sea
His overcoat for ever,
And wears the turning globe.

or:

Stay, O sweet, and do not rise!
The light that shines comes from thine eyes;
The day breaks not: it is my heart,
Because that you and I must part.
Stay! or else my joys will die
And perish in their infancy.

Thomas Hardy's poetry, especially, contains many examples of accidental metaphor of this kind. It is true that passion, as we find it expressed in the language of poetry, *can* transcend the limits of the personal without at the same time rising to knowledge and so creating true metaphor. But in this case, it seems not so much to *expand* our consciousness, as to strip us of all that is accidental and trivial and thus identify us in some way with the core of all human *feeling*. Consequently, it has no room for accidental and fanciful metaphors, nor, indeed, for any kind of metaphor, but achieves its end by absolute simplicity and directness of diction:

> *Quand vous serez bien vieille, au soir à la chandelle*
> *Assise auprès du feu, devidant et filant,*
> *Direz, chantant mes vers, en vous émerveillant,*
> *Ronsard me célébroit du temps que j'étais belle.*

Burns's most perfect lines supply us with any number of further examples. Those, however, who place undue emphasis on this element in their judgements of poetry (e.g. in preferring the *Inferno* to the *Paradiso*) forget—as Croce pointed out—the distinction between passion as matter and passion as form. Whereas it is precisely when it is transmuted, and as it were frozen into form, that passion becomes most truly aesthetic.

That, in the post-logical period, accidental metaphors have found their way into the current meanings of words, if anything, more easily than the true is apparent from etymology.[1] Nor is this surprising. For from what has been said (Appendix II) we can very easily see that this kind of metaphor is based on *a synthesis of ideas*, rather than on immediate cognition of reality. And since all words are, as we have seen, obliged to express general notions, the false metaphor is naturally more adapted to the dictionary meaning of a word than the true.

[1] E.g. *bank, cancel, centre, calculus, foible, govern, muscle, size.* etc. Those which look like true metaphors are nearly all old words, whose meanings have divided (IV, 1 and 2). It seems that true metaphors usually affect language too subtly to have an etymological, in addition to a semantic, effect.

[2]

It will frequently be found, in the case of accidental metaphors, that the *sphere* of the analogy can be precisely limited or named in some way; as when Mercutio describes Queen Mab as being

In shape no bigger than an agate-stone
On the forefinger of an alderman

where the comparison can be named as one of *size*, or in such simple, everyday metaphors as the use of a *couple* or a *brace* for 'two', where the idea of 'twoness' has evidently been first abstracted and then re-clothed in imagery. In fact, the accidental metaphor generally carries with it a suggestion of having been constructed upon a sort of framework of logic. This kind Aristotle in the *Poetics* calls κατὰ τὸ ἀνάλογον,[1] and the example he gives is 'the shield of Bacchus', which describes a cup, because 'a cup is to Bacchus what a shield is to Ares'. Now, while it is no doubt true that all metaphors can be *reduced* to the mathematical ratio $a:b::c:d$, they ought not to give the sense of having been constructed on it; and where that is so, we may probably assume that the *real* relation between the two images is but exiguous and remote, the remainer of the resemblance being accidental. In this respect Example V(*a*) is perhaps inferior, as true metaphor, to V(*b*), where a very great deal of abstraction is necessary before we can arrive at the ratio: 'my experience of you is to the rest of my experience as the sun is to the earth'.

[1] *Poetics*, 21.

[3]

The distinction between true and false metaphor corresponds to the distinction between Myth and Allegory, allegory being a more or less conscious hypostatization of *ideas* (Appendix II, 6), followed by a synthesis of them, and myth the true child of Meaning, begotten on imagination. There is no doubt that, from a very early date, the Greek poets began to mix false metaphor with their original myths, just as the Greek philosophers began to contaminate them with allegory; so that in this case the form in which the myths have come down to us it itself dual.

The modern poet has created a new myth or made a true use of an old one, according as the myth in question is the direct embodiment of concrete experience and not of his *idea* of that experience—in which case he has only invented an allegory, or made an allegorical use of a myth, as the case may be.

[4]

The famous distinction between Fancy and Imagination was evidently drawn by Coleridge, because he divined the accidental, merely *personal*, nature of the synthetic metaphors of fancy, and yet was convinced of the concrete reality of others. Imagination, by which these latter are begotten, he called—in that extraordinary, unfinished XIIIth chapter of the *Biographia Literaria*—'esemplastic' (see Appendix II, 4). Referring to this distinction, Mr. Lascelles Abercrombie, in *The Idea of Great Poetry*, remarks that 'the faculty of fancy does not exist; it is one of Coleridge's chimeras, of which he kept a whole stable. Fancy is nothing but a degree of imagination.'

Now this is only true in the sense that every 'chimera' in Coleridge's or any other brain is itself a 'degree' of universal reality, and therefore does not differ 'in kind' from a polar-bear or a toothbrush. The objection to the rarefied Eleatic standpoint, which reduces all 'kinds' to 'degrees', is not its falsity, but its inutility—except as an occasional intellectual exercise. On the contrary, the distinction between Fancy and Imagination is one which ought to be particularly emphasized in an age like ours, divorced from reality by universal abstraction of thought, and in which the fanciful poetry of 'escape', as it is sometimes called, is so popular.

'Escape', in this sense, is clearly from an unpleasant, which is conceived as real, to a pleasant, which is conceived as unreal. It is thus analogous to taking opium, or getting drunk. And it is the tragedy of art in our time that most of those who—whether they desire it or not—are regarded as the living representatives of the poetic, are under the spell of a Kantian conception of knowledge, or, worse still, a popular conception of 'Science'. Consequently, even those who give much of their time to reading, yes, and writing about, the greatest poetry, frequently reveal their sense of its 'unreality' as compared with the rest of the life about them. Where will it end? When the real is taken as unreal, and the unreal as real, the road is open to the madhouse.

APPENDIX IV

SUBJECTIVE AND OBJECTIVE

[1]

Opposed to the naturalistic explanation of myth which was briefly criticized in IV, 4, there is, as was hinted at the time, that rather more modern idea, which is summed up in the word *animism*. From this point of view—worked up into some detail, on psycho-analytical lines, by Jung and others—the myths are seen as a sort of unconscious 'projection' of the inner life of feeling and impulse upon an inanimate outer world. Now whenever this excellent word 'projection' is spoken or thought, the humble student of meaning feels inclined to join the devotees of another, more popular, amusement: he makes his bow to an ingenious little machine which was christened by our simple-minded forefathers 'magic lantern'. For the curious idea of 'projection' which this invention begot in us, is now nearly as ubiquitous as its grosser offspring, the cinema. We see it applied daily, with the greatest success. Take early Greek philosophy, for instance: this is now known to have been actually an inquiry into the nature of knowledge, although *it thought itself to be* an inquiry into the nature of *Being*! And this is because it *projected* its subjective intellectual processes on to the objective world of mechanical causes and effects.

The refutation of this notion of projected subjectivity, as applied to the history of consciousness, is a simple one, and is really implicit in the concept of 'logomorphism' which I tried to convey in Chapter IV, 4. It is simply that, at the time when the myths came into being, our distinction between subjective and objective cannot have existed. A subjective—or *self*—consciousness is inseparable, as Kant himself demonstrated quite satisfactorily, from rational or discursive thought operating in abstract ideas. Consequently, in pre-logical times it could not have existed at all. Any 'projecting' which may be necessary, therefore, is done by the modern theorist himself, not in space but in time; and the picture projected—strangely enough—is a picture of a man with a magic lantern.

The only way of avoiding the somewhat subtle traps which are constantly laid for us by logomorphism is to accustom ourselves thoroughly to the thought that the dualism, *objective: subjective*, is fundamental neither psychologically, historically, nor philosophically. I pause here again for emphasis. For now we are at the very heart of the matter. We are confronting that inveterate habit of thought which makes it so extraordinarily hard for the Western mind to grasp the nature of inspiration. From the birth of Nominalism in the Dark Ages down to our own day, the habit has been taking a firmer and firmer grip, with the result that a conception, which in the East is, or was, merely the threshold—the *pons asinorum*—of any serious thinking at all, has in the West been long reserved to the intuitive grasp of a few more or less neglected mystics. I cannot now develop this at length, but I wish in conclusion to make a very few remarks under each of the above heads, if only to the extent of indicating sources to which the reader could go himself, in order to study the matter further on these lines.

(i) For a treatment of the genesis of subjectivity in the development of the individual human being, he is again referred to the psychological work of Professor J. M. Baldwin,[1] who has traced, albeit in a somewhat obscure and difficult style, the development of the child from this point of view. Thus, he endeavours to show how, at first an 'individual' only in the bodily sense, the child draws, as it were, its subjectivity out of perception and thought:

'The individual learns to treat his own body as a tool for turning all the series of external things into copy for his mental manipulation. He thus achieves the wonderful step whereby all objects alike become *his* objects, *his* content of meaning, *his* experience.'[2]

Gradually, through, and out of, a simple distinction of *inner* from *outer*, there arises the dualism, *self: not-self*, the constituents of which two conceptions will still continue to change their places with the increase of knowledge and self-knowledge. *Before* this stage, a logical mode of intellection is impossible; back to it can be traced a 'quasi-logical' mode, comprising 'the objective constructions which intervene before the rise of the distinction of self and its experience'. *Meaning*, on the contrary, is something which in no sense depends from, but *includes*, all these laboriously acquired distinctions.

[1] *Handbook of Psychology; Mental Development in the Child and the Race; Thought and Things*. Especially the last. [2] *Thought and Things* i, , V, 7.

'We cannot say that the derivation of meanings follows from the distinction of inner and outer, or self and not-self. On the contrary, *these latter are themselves meanings*.'[1]

(ii) I believe that a reasonably sensitive, and at the same time unprejudiced, examination of the semantic histories of words, must of itself lead to the conclusion that the distinction of objective from subjective is a relatively late arrival in human consciousness. Some of my reasons for supposing this are apparent from the text. In a small book *History in English Words*, I endeavoured to trace, as far as was possible within the limits of a popular work attempting to cover a large area, some semantic indications of this process in its later stages. For example, it was shown there that the distinction in question, though it must of course have been developing before, did not rise to the level of philosophic consciousness until the time of the Stoic sect.[2]

This is why, in order to form a conception of the consciousness of primitive man, we have really—as I suggested—as it were, to '*unthink*', not merely our now half-instinctive logical processes, but even the seemingly fundamental distinction between self and world. And with this, the distinction between thinking and perceiving begins to vanish too.[3] For perception, unlike the pure concept, is inconceivable without a distinct perceiving subject on which the percepts, the soul-and sense-data, can impinge. Consequently for Locke's picture of Adam at work on the synthetic manufacture of language[4] we have to substitute —what? A kind of thinking which is at the same time per-

[1] *Ibid.*, i, VII, 9.
[2] See also Rudolf Eucken's *Geschichte der Philosophischen Terminologie.*
[3] Cf. IV, 3
[4] Appendix II, 2.

ceiving—a picture-thinking, a figurative, or imaginative, consciousness, which we can only grasp today by true analogy with the imagery of our poets, and, to some extent, with our own dreams.

From the very nature of it, it follows that the period during which this type of consciousness prevailed in its fullness must have been *pre*-historic. The earliest written documents, and the early state of our languages, will consequently point us back to, without revealing, it. The revelation itself is left to our own imaginative reconstruction, the extent of which will depend upon individual ability and effort.[1] And here the reader is once more referred to the voluminous writings of Rudolf Steiner, who brought to bear upon precisely this ancient consciousness an amazing wealth of intuition, inspiration, and imagination, illuminating it out of an inexhaustible fertility in metaphor with a brilliant flood of poetic light.

It may conceivably be objected at this point that the progress of language, etc., only indicates a growing *consciousness* of the subjective-objective dualism, which was always there in reality, though men did not know it. Such an objection, however, would be meaningless; for the words, subjective and objective, have no reference except to consciousness. The thought at the back of the objector's mind would, thus, probably be that human being always involved a number of *bodies more or less detached from the rest of the physical world*: but this has nothing whatever to do with subjectivity, except as a possible means to it. Or again, the objection might be raised that such a state of

[1] Spengler points out, refreshingly, that even recorded history is really only accessible to cognition in which the poetic predominates.

consciousness is necessarily inconceivable to beings who are themselves subjectively organized, so that all talk about it is no more than an idle flapping of wings. This brings us face to face with the whole paradox of knowledge and inspiration.

(iii) It was said in Appendix II (§ 5), by way of comment on the *Critique of Pure Reason*, that it is not justifiable, in constructing a theory of knowledge, to take subjectivity as 'given'. Why? Because, if we examine the thinking activity carefully, by subsequent reflection on it, we shall find that in the *act* of thinking, or knowing, no such distinction of consciousness exists. We are not conscious of ourselves thinking about something, but simply of something. The dualism only arises later, when the particular thought has been associated, in me, with some part of my perceptual world, whether inner or outer (sense or feeling), and has thus taken on the form of an *idea*—my idea. The case is quite different with feeling. Consequently, in thinking about thinking, if we are determined to make no assumptions at the outset, we dare not start with the distinction of self and not-self; for that distinction actually disappears every time we think. For a very full discussion of all this, I have no choice but to point yet again to Steiner, who in several of his books has treated the whole subject with great skill and delicacy:

'Thinking must never be regarded as a merely subjective activity. Thinking transcends the distinction of subject and object. It produces these two concepts just as it produces all others. When, therefore, I, as thinking subject, refer a concept to an object, we must not regard this reference as something purely subjective. It is not the subject, but thought, which makes the reference. The subject does not think because it is a subject, rather it conceives itself to be a subject because it can think. The activity of consciousness, in so far as it thinks, is thus not merely subjective. Rather it is neither subjective nor objective; it transcends both these concepts. I ought never to say that I, as individual subject, think, but rather that I, as subject, exist myself by the grace of thought.'[1]

Thus, the problem of inspiration, depicted in Chapter VI, 3, again reveals itself as identical in essence with the problem of knowledge itself. In the moment of knowing, which is also the real moment of poetic creation, the knower ceases to exist as subject at all; and, conversely, when he comes fully to himself, as subject, he ceases to know. Imaginations are generated in his consciousness as he passes from the former state to the latter, and the difficulty is, of course, to retain them in some form in the memory. The analogy with dreaming is here very exact; for everybody knows how the dream, which seemed vivid in every detail, while we were still only half-conscious, may vanish altogether during the last minute that is spent in waking right up. The special faculty needed to overcome this paradox of inspiration has been described, with effective accuracy, as '*presence* of mind'.

More loosely, it may be presented as the problem of *memory*. How, and in what form, to carry over into the uninspired *self*-consciousness some *memory* of that other inspired consciousness, which to the unpoetic man is not consciousness at all but sleep—that selfless moment when, as Wordsworth wrote in the *Prelude*, 'the light of sense

[1] *The Philosophy of Spiritual Activity*, pp. 51–2.

goes out'? How to do this, when memory itself is unthinkable without sense? Thus, we find Aristotle saying of the poetic (ποιητικός) mind, that *we do not remember*;[1] we find the mystics imbued with a pregnant sense of war between Memory and Inspiration; and Dante, after the final supreme vision of 'La forma universal', adds that the lapse of a single moment plunged that vision into greater oblivion than twenty-five centuries could produce in the case of an ordinary event.[2]

Such, then, is the paradox of inspiration. The time-honoured 'subjective-objective' dichotomy vanishes in the light of concrete thinking; and the word *concrete* can perhaps best be defined as 'that which is neither objective nor subjective'. Because I have used the word *meaning* in a similar manner, the objection may be raised by those who are not willing to follow me in this Appendix that I have used it in two different senses. In actual fact this is not so. Finally, as regards the two 'principles' which were described to some extent in IV, 3, and have been referred to throughout, these must themselves be conceived concretely.

The Greeks had no such word as 'principle'; they called what I have been speaking of—with that divine concreteness which makes the mere language a fountain of strength

[1] *De Anima*, III, 5 (see p. xi)

[2] *Paradiso*, XXXIII, 91:

> *La forma universal di questo nodo*
> *credo ch' io vidi, perchè più di largo,*
> *dicendo questo, mi sento ch' io godo.*
>
> *Un punto solo m' è maggior letargo,*
> *che venticinque secoli alla impresa,*
> *che fe' Nettuno ammirar l' ombra d' Argo.*

for the exhausted modern intelligence—simply ποιεῖν and πάσχειν—Do and Suffer.

But to ordinary abstract thought a *principle* can never be anything more than an *idea*, induced from observations of what *has* happened. I used the word because I wished to proceed inductively as far as was possible to the subject in hand, having myself, as I believe, arrived in that manner at the necessity for supposing such principles. Yet all conclusions of this nature could be no more than subjective shadows of the forces themselves, of the two living realities, which can actually be *known*, once our intellect has brought us to the point of looking out for them; being themselves neither subjective nor objective, but as concrete and self-sustaining in every way as the Sun and the Moon—which may well be their proper names.

AFTERWORD

The Preface to the second edition (1952) was mainly a discussion of the opposite point of view. It was preoccupied with those whom I will call "enemies" for short, though I am not aware of much personal animosity. This is also true to a considerable extent of the book itself.

Poetic Diction was first published in 1928 and, in so far as it is philosophically argumentative, notably in the second and fourth appendices, the enemies were Locke, Kant and the post-Kantian subjective idealists. By 1952 subjective idealism had gone out of fashion and the enemy was Logical Positivism, a school of thought which acknowledged a greater debt to Hume than to either Locke or Kant. It is obvious enough that the Preface was written at about the time of the transition from Logical Positivism to Linguistic Analysis, or at all events at about the time when I became aware of it. It is dated 1951, twenty-three years after the book itself was published, and in it I was rash enough to utter two prophecies — first, that "after the lapse of another twenty-three years the particular doctrines of linguistic analysis are unlikely to be a very live issue". Twenty-one of them have now elapsed, and I do not think I can honestly claim that the prophecy has been fulfilled. Of course a good deal depends on what is meant by the word "live", but if I adopted that line of defence, I should be rather driven to contend that it never has been live. That might not be so difficult; on the other hand, if "live" is taken to mean "enjoying publicity", I must confess, though this particular "enemy" is now enjoying a good deal less of it, that the prophecy was a rash one.

I added (and this was the second prophecy) that

> If I seem to have given them [the particular doctrines of linguistic analysis] disproportionate attention, it is because they are, to my mind, the typical contemporary outcrop of a subterranean view of human response which is itself unlikely to peter out. On the contrary the conflicting theories of knowledge of which the following pages take cognizance show every sign of diverging more and more widely, leaving a deeper and deeper gulf of incomprehension between them. Between those for whom 'knowledge' means ignorant but effective power, and those for whom the individual imagination is the medium of all knowledge from perception upward, a truce will not readily be struck.

This prophecy was a long-term one, and I doubt if a retrospect of only twenty-one years has much evidential value one way or the other. To say the least of it however, I see few signs that it is *not* being fulfilled. This is not the place to say anything of the gulf at its sociological level — the virtual breakdown of communication between the devotees of technocracy on one side and the habitual lovers of nature and life on the other. But, on the level of discourse, so far as I have been able to ascertain by enquiry, it is a fact that almost everyone with a spark of life in his mind has long been finding the whole riddle-me-ree of analytical linguistics tedious to the point of extinction, while we in our turn are seen by its exponents as dwellers beyond the pale in some nameless abyss of empty verbiage. More perhaps than ever before it is the case that, as Coleridge put it,

> there is many a one among us, yes, and some who think themselves philosophers too, to whom the philosophic organ is entirely wanting. To such a man philosophy is a mere play of words and notions, like a theory of music to the deaf, or like the geometry of light to the blind.

But it is also the case that there are many for whom philosophy is (again in Coleridge's words) "the mind's self-experience in the act of thinking". When the question was raised of yet another Preface being written for this reprinting, it was decided for typographical reasons that an Afterword would be better. And I propose to use it for speaking finally, not of the "enemies", of whom, incidentally, I am thoroughly tired, but of "friends" instead. There are many of them, and even at the time I was writing the book there were very many more than I knew.

To take one instance, Ernst Cassirer's *Philosophy of Symbolic Forms* appeared in Germany over the period 1923–1929, and it was not the first of his many books. I am not sure when they first began to appear in English or if any other had done so before Susanne Langer translated *Language and Myth* in 1946. In one of her own books,

Feeling and Form (1953), Miss Langer devoted a few paragraphs to a comparison between Cassirer's conception of the nature of language and my own in *Poetic Diction*, in the course of which she remarked of a particular passage that "it could almost pass for a paraphrase of Cassirer's *Language and Myth* . . . fragments from the *Philosophie der Symbolischen Formen*"; and she added, "the parallel is so striking that it is hard to believe in its pure coincidence, yet such it seems to be". Such it certainly was, since at the time I wrote *Poetic Diction*, I did not know German and had never heard of Cassirer.

Naturally I heard of him later on and studied many of his writings with admiration, pleasure and profit. But if there was a very good reason why I had not come across Cassirer, the same can hardly be said of F. M. Cornford's *From Religion to Philosophy*, a book which was published as long ago as 1912 and which seems to me to parallel in a no less striking way the general picture of an evolution from concrete to abstract thinking which *Poetic Diction* tries to present.

Perhaps these instances will suffice to illustrate the fact that there were already not just two or three, but many more friends about than I knew of. The number is much greater of those who have come to the fore since 1928. To attempt anything approaching a survey would take too long and is probably beyond my powers. The most I can do is to mention a few of the names that come to my mind, or that can be brought to it with the help of old and untidy notes out of the desultory reading I have been able to do since my book was written. I should perhaps add that, for personal reasons, most of that has taken place during the last fifteen years or so, though of course it was not confined to books published within that period. So many books moreover are written in our time that I suspect the omissions will be at least as important as the selection.

On the topic of metaphor, from a consideration of which the whole argument of *Poetic Diction* is developed, I recall the appearance in 1936 of W. Bedell Stanford's *Greek Metaphor,* which was perhaps the earliest of many careful studies of the subject, and with which I tend to associate both Bruno Snell's *Discovery of the Mind*, because of its admirable chapter on Homer's diction, and R. B. Onians's *The Origins of European Thought,* which is likewise specially concerned with the Greek language. I also take this opportunity to mention a little known book by Thorlief Boman, *Hebrew Thought Compared with Greek*, which was published in German in 1954 and in English by the Students Christian Movement Press in 1960. More generally no one who is interested in the subject should overlook its development, including the invention of some useful terminology, in such books as *Metaphor and Reality* and *The Burning Fountain*, written by the late Philip Wheelwright before his tragically early death a few years ago.

The "making of meaning", as it is here called, is a subject which has been attracting attention from more than one direction. One of these is the place of symbol and image in poetry, in literature generally and in language itself. To mention C. Day Lewis's *The Poetic Image* is to select one out of a very large number of thoughtful books and essays, and the subject has been tentatively explored by many critics who have written on the Romantic Movement. For a representative selection of the latter I should be inclined to recommend Harold Bloom's anthology *Romanticism and Consciousness* (1970). In a larger perspective we have had Auerbach's *Mimesis*, and particularly the part of it included under the title of "Figura" in his *Scenes from the Drama of European Literature*. But neither symbolism nor meaning can be confined to literature, or even to language, and it would be misleading to omit such adventurous explorers in the field of "iconology" as Edgar Wind and E. H. Gombrich, especially as their findings bring out so clearly that relation between symbolical expression and perception itself, which was the next step, so to speak, in the argument of this book.

The view that human perception is not simply the reception of impacts on the physical organism, but involves an unconscious *activity* of the mind, is at least as old as Coleridge's "primary imagination". But I would say that it is much more widespread today than it was in 1928 or even in 1952, owing to the amount of attention which precisely that activity has been receiving. Donald Davie's *Articulate Energy* may serve for an example. Something like a *genetic* psychology is now perhaps taken for granted by most people to whom imagination is more than a word, whereas in Victorian times E. S. Dallas (author of *The Gay Science*, with its chapter on "The Hidden Soul") was an unregarded voice crying in the wilderness. That that activity has a cognitive as well as an aesthetic function is also being vigorously maintained in many quarters. I find myself thinking in that connection of Cassirer once more, of L. L. Whyte and, particularly in relation to language, of Benjamin Whorf. Not that there are no others. Before 1928 there was nothing like M. H. Abrams's admirable *The Mirror and the Lamp* for a young man to feed his mind on, while at the same time absorbing a detailed history of the Romantic Movement. The steady growth of interest in Coleridge's prose alone has produced a rich crop of sympathetic articles as well as a number of books, of which by far the most outstanding is Paul Deschamps's *La Formation de la Pensée de Coleridge* (1964).

But it is argued in *Poetic Diction* not merely that that activity exists, but that it has developed; that, in addition to the history of ideas, there is a history of consciousness or, let us say, a history of the whole mind including its unconscious part — so that, if Collingwood's definition of "history" (all real *history* is history of thought) is accepted, the term "evolution" of consciousness is perhaps more satisfactory. This, though not widely accepted, can no longer be called an unfamiliar notion. It is a recognisable stream of theory, which can be seen as the convergence of a number of separate tributaries. The so-called "psychology of the unconscious" — Jung's archetypes and his "pre-logical" period, Freud's essay on the *Antithetical Sense of Primal Words* — is one of them. Maud Bodkin's first book *Archetypal Patterns in Poetry* goes back to 1934, but since then and extending beyond the confines of literature, I have noticed, for instance, Erich Neumann's *The Origins and History of Consciousness* and Van den Berg's *The Changing Nature of Man*.

Another tributary has been preoccupation with myth and subsidiarily with dream: Leslie Fiedler's essay *Myth and Signature*, Mircea Éliade, Gaston Bachelard, Northrop

Frye, the publications of the Society for Arts, Religion and Culture, such as *Interpretation: the Poetry of Meaning* and *Myth, Dream and Religion.* I have aimed, in the last few pages, at some sort of division under separate heads, but the categories overlap too much for it to have been of much use. The two volumes last mentioned could almost as well have been cited on the topic of metaphor; Snell's *Discovery of the Mind* is at least as relevant to this paragraph as it was to the one in which it was included.

It would be an even more fatal weakness to omit in this connection Elizabeth Sewell's *The Orphic Voice* (1964), which also has the advantage of carrying me a little further on in the sort of thing I wish to say — for, on this subject, it is not only among contemporary or relatively recent writers that "friends" are distinguishable from "enemies". There are also the older writers, who may be called the classics of the doctrine of living spirit rather than inanimate matter or energy as the ultimate source of human consciousness. I still recall rather vividly the surprise, slightly tinged with embarrassment, with which, a few years after it was written, the highly original author of *Poetic Diction* learned that early in the eighteenth century a man called Giambattista Vico had propounded something he called "sapienza poetica" as the earliest form of human thought.[1] It may be profitably compared and contrasted with the "collective representations" of which some anthropologists,

[1] Rather oddly, Coleridge reports a similar experience. To an Italian correspondent, who had sent him Vico's *Scienza Nuova*, he wrote in 1825: "I am more and more delighted with G. B. Vico, and if I had . . . the least drop of *Author's* blood in my veins, I should twenty times successively in the perusal of the first volume . . . have exclaimed: *Pereant qui ante nos nostra dixere.*"

notably Lévy-Bruhl, began to speak about a hundred years later.

But I am thinking now of a rather different heritage. By the classics of the subject I mean more especially that recognisable but loosely defined line of thinkers for whom the only generic term that has so far been found is "Neo-Platonists". That it *is* a line, or rather say a stream, of thought, and not simply a string of isolated oddities, who got born somehow in order to borrow from and influence each other, has itself been a discovery marking the last few decades. They have given us, perhaps outstandingly but far from exclusively, Cassirer's *The Platonic Renaissance in England*, Wind's *Pagan Mysteries in the Renaissance*, Arthur Lovejoy's *The Great Chain of Being*, Frances Yates's two books *Bruno and the Hermetic Tradition* and the *Art of Memory* and in 1968 Kathleen Raine's *Blake and Tradition*. It is her awareness of the stream *as* a stream, from the Orphic tradition to Goethe and the *Naturphilosophen* which gives to Elizabeth Sewell's book, already referred to above, its peculiar strength and value. Finally, in the spring of this year M. H. Abrams bestowed upon us in his *Natural Supernaturalism,* with an understanding hardly less sympathetic though more detached than that of Miss Sewell, the most thoroughly systematic exploration we have yet seen of the Neo-Platonic tradition considered from the point of view of its culmination in Romantic literature and philosophy.

There has perhaps been no better characterisation of the distinction between Platonism *tout simple* and Neo-Platonism than was made by whoever defined the latter as "Platonism plus the concept of genius". At all events it seems to me to be in this sense that the stream of thought to which I have referred may properly be termed "Neo-Platonic". Plotinus, Plutarch, Iamblichus, Synesius, Augustine, Ficino, Bruno, Boehme, Henry More, Shaftesbury, Blake, Goethe, Coleridge, Emerson and Yeats were no doubt very unlike each other in many respects; but they were all aware, in a way that Pythagoras and Plato were not yet aware, of the active role of individual human spirit.

It was not only of Frances Cornford, Cassirer and Vico that I was ignorant when I wrote *Poetic Diction.* I was equally ignorant of almost all that I have just been saying. But I will add, to redress the balance a little on the scales of humility, that I sometimes wonder whether this may not have proved rather an advantage. If the book does anything, it erects a structure of thought on the basis of a felt difference between what it calls "the Prosaic" and "the Poetic". Corollary thereto is a further distinction drawn between two kinds of poetry, or of the Poetic itself, and further the conception that that distinction reveals human consciousness as in process of evolution. And I wonder if the fact that I seemed to have discovered, or rather to be discovering, these things for myself, mainly by pondering the felt difference to which I have referred, may not have imparted a certain energy that accounts for its having apparently outlasted some other books by men who knew a great deal more both of literature and of the history of ideas. I am careful to say "seemed", in order to scotch any mistaken notion that I am still covertly claiming some sort of first-that-ever-burst discovery on the lines of stout Cortez; nor should I be specially surprised to learn that even the *re*discovery was less empirical than I supposed, and that something written by someone like Cornford (I expect there are others of whom I still·do not know) had belletristically filtered through to me and been forgotten. More important, I had the advantage of having at least begun an acquaintance with the work of Rudolf Steiner, so that, if I knew nothing of the past history of the stream, I was tasting its present waters. I referred to this in the first Preface and everything said there I would now repeat, only with greater emphasis. It is very evident that there is also the opposite possibility — of becoming so engrossed in the excitement of map-reading oneself back to the "sources" that one omits altogether the formality of kneeling and taking a sip.

It should be noted that *Poetic Diction* does not simply exalt the Poetic at the expense of the Prosaic, but emphasises their essential relation, their dependence on each other, and indeed their interpenetration. That is, incidentally, the significance of the epigraph quoted from Coleridge. By contrast much else that had been written before and has been written since has been directed to stressing an inreconcilable antagonism between the two. "Codlin's the friend, not Short" is the burden of most books and essays on the nature of poetry and the Poetic. This I take to be the symptom in the literary sphere of a weakness common to pretty well all the "friends" to whom I have referred, whether their sphere is aesthetics, psychology, anthropology, the significance of myth or the history of Neo-Platonism. It is that at the bottom of it all they do not quite believe their own brave words. Jung, for instance, speaks of a collective Unconscious, of Archetypes, of "primordial images"; and Maud Bodkin quotes him; and Day Lewis quotes Maud Bodkin quoting him; and it turns out that those Archetypes are "psychic residua of numberless experiences of the same type". Just how primordial is a residuum? The truth is, it is not possible to speak convincingly of the active role of the individual human spirit in the world, while you continue to feel in your bones, whatever your intellect may be saying to you, that the individual human spirit is something that is encased in an individual human body. It was when this encapsulation began to be the general experience of humanity that the stream of Platonism, though it did not cease, became, as Neo-Platonism, an underground stream, and philosophically no longer quite respectable.

The common experience today is of world and mind as things totally heterogeneous to one another. Theoretical reconciliations take the form of making one swallow the other. Either you are a materialist, and all is really matter; or you are an idealist, and all is really mind. Whichever of the two you adopt, you will not really believe it, because it will not be borne out by your behaviour. But to take the Poetic really seriously is another matter. It is not to slang the Prosaic, and with it the whole world of science and technology, as the French Symbolists did, and hide yourself away in an ivory tower of "art". It is to begin work on the interpenetration of the two by seeking to overcome in a man's own experience what Coleridge termed the "outness" of the phenomenal world. To say that this involves experiencing that world and his own individual spirit, not as other, but as "opposite" is perhaps to say something. It is indeed to say what Coleridge said.

But here perhaps more than anywhere else it is the case that mere acceptance of a proposition is almost nothing. "It is not enough", as he remarked in another context, "that we have once swallowed it — the *Heart* should have *fed* upon the *truth*, as insects on a leaf — till it be tinged with its colour and show its food in even the minutest fibre". I have no means of knowing about their hearts, but as far as their writings are concerned, I seem to myself to have detected more of that "tinging" in the utterances of one or two physicists, such as Werner Heisenberg or David Bohm, than anywhere in the humanities. I doubt if this is an accident. There is much work still to be done in revealing the part played by that underground stream in the development of modern science. Kepler is an obvious example, but we also need a new and unbiased biography of Isaac Newton and a study, not based on *petitio principii*, of such matters as the relation between alchemy and chemistry, astrology and astronomy. There was a time, and quite a long one, before we had learned to call that experienced heterogeneity scientific "method" and, with its consequential increase, to substitute closed-mindedness for open-mindedness as the criterion of the scientific "spirit".

But these are considerations I have struggled to deal with elsewhere. Pray what is "spirit"? Is it one, or many, or both at the same time? Is it always good, or sometimes not so good? In the second Preface I suggested that "today the study of poetry and of the poetic element in all meaningful language is a valuable exercise for other purposes than the practice or better enjoyment of poetry". If this is so (and I could perhaps claim Heidegger on Hölderlin as bearing it out), it is so by virtue of the fact that poetry, where it exists at all, exists not by affirming but by actually experiencing, however slightly, the ultimate homogeneity of world and mind. Of course there must be a genuine love of poetry in the first place; for otherwise it would not *be* poetry a man was studying, but something else. The heart must be in it as well as the head, if it is to feed on the truth. If so, as the study proceeds and if it remains faithful to the experience, then as the insect begins to take the colour of the leaf in every minutest fibre, the head is led on to a better understanding, not only of the Poetic, but of the Prosaic as well. And it discovers that it is not the opposite of poetry, but its contradiction, which is the "enemy". To borrow Pascal's terminology it is not "geometry" but the *spirit* of geometry which declares war on "the spirit of finesse".

South Darenth, Kent OWEN BARFIELD
August 1972

INDEX

ABERCROMBIE, Lascelles, 201
Accent, 150
Addison, 128–9
Aesthetic :
dist. from *Poetic*, 170, 178–9
synthesis, 189 *et seq.*
Allegory, 123
dist. from *Myth*, 201
Appreciation (see *Contemplation*)
of Nature, 182
Archaism, 179
defined, 163, 165
literary and *colloquial* 163 *et seq.*
Aristotle, 61, 62, 95, 108 n, 132, 140, 141 n, 171, 191, 200, 210
Art, 50, 140, 150, 151, 182
and *the Prosaic*, 169
and *knowledge*, 194–5, 202

BACON, Francis, 86, 87 n, 135, 137, 140, 141–2, 158
Baldwin, J. M, 82, 142, 205
Ballads, 43, 50
Barstow, M. L., 162, 183 n
Blair, Hugh, 72, 73 n, 85
Blake, William, 113 n, 144
Boiardo, 114 n
Botany, 176, 190
Bradley, Henry, 154–6
Bréal, M., 69 n, 73 n, 133–4, 153, 156–7

CAMPION, Thomas, 43–4, 51
Change :
Aesthetic pleasure depends on, 48, 52, *et seq*, 57, 69, 152, 162
Chaucer, 51, 98, 172
Chesterton, G. K., 174
Chinese Language, 78, 99, 144, 149, 156
Coleridge, 58, 101, 135, 180, 191, 201–2
'*Collector*', the, 139–40, 169
Concept, (see *Meaning*, *Idea*, *Percept*)
Concrete (see *Meaning*)
defined, 210
Consciousness (see *Change*, '*Given*')
defined, 48
'primitive', 48–9, 65, 73–4, 78–81, 84 *et seq.*, 93, 102–107, 111, 113, 142–3, 146–7 ,187, 203–8
Contemplation (see *Creation*), 152
excludes *Creation*, 49, 102 *et seq.*
Conversation :
and Prose, 164
Creation defined, 112
excludes *contemplation*, 49, 51, 102 *et seq.*, 107–8, 159–60, 167, 169–70
Criticism and Critics, 53–4, 132, 166–70
personal element in, 42, 58–9
confidence of genuine, 70, 89, 92
Croce, Benedetto, 140, 184, 194–5, 199

DANTE, 58, 95, 108, 148, 199, 210
and Latin, 165
Davison, E. L., 125
Definition, 62, 131, 133, 187, 191
de la Mare, Walter, 157
Dickens, Charles, 176

Index

Discovery, 138, 142
Dreams, 52, 207, 209
Dryden, 121, 130, 164, 175
Du Bellay, 58, 165

EMERSON, 92, 108, 179
English Literature, 58, 96–98 116 *et seq.*, 147
Etymology (see *Philology*)

FANCY, 123
  and *Imagination*, 135, 201–2
Fashion, poetic, 162–3, 166–7
Feeling, 13, 198–9
Figurative nature of primitive language, 72 *et seq.*, 78–9, 85, 88–9, 134
  dist. from 'figure of speech', 88
  Consciousness, 206–7
France, Anatole, 64, 65, 75, 79, 84, 86
French Literature, 152–3, 165–6, 172

GERMAN Language, 155
Gibbon, 104
'*Given*' meaning, 102, 108, 111, 114–6, 133, 140, 146–7, 179
Goethe, 91, 140
Goldsmith, Oliver, 127–8
Grammar and *Grammarians*, 60, 81–2, 98, 131, 149, 153 *et seq.*
Gray, Thomas, 123, 152–3, 164 166 n, 172
Greek Language, 60–1, 64, 69, 79–80, 93–4, 96–8, 133, 210–11

HARDY, Thomas, 198
Hegel, 111, 145 n
Herbert, George, 173–4
Hobbes, Thomas, 138, 185
Homer, 69, 70, 71–2, 93–4, 97–8, 104, 105–6
Horace, 98, 116, 131

IDEA, 48–9, 190–1, 208, 211
  and *Percept*, 190, 193–4
  and *Concept*, 193–5
  hypostatized, 195–6, 201
Imagination, 70 n, 141, 180
  defined, 41
  discussed, 47 *et seq.*
  Fancy and, 135, 201–2
  'esemplastic', 191, 201
  = individualized Poetic, 144, 191
  knowledge accessible only to, 95 n, 133, 138–9, 143–4, 188, 207, 207 n
  Kant on, 192
Imaginative consciousness, 206–7, 209
Inspiration, 109, 113, 141, 169–70, 189–90, 208 *et seq.*,
  opposed to *Memory*, 209–10
'*Interpreter*', the, 132, 160–70
Intuition, 133, 193 n

JESPERSEN, Otto, 78, 84, 99–101, 155
Johnson, Dr., 175, 180

KANT, 183 *et seq.*, 204
  influence of, 75, 184, 194–5, 196, 202, 208
Keats, 108, 180
Kepler, 138
Knowledge, 55, 57, 70, 106, 139, 141 *et seq.*, 160, 163, 166 n, 171, 183 *et seq.*, 199, 208 *et seq.*

LAMB, Charles, 159
Language :
  history and 'progress' of, 57–8, 62 *et seq.*, 93 *et seq.*, 99 *et seq.*, 144, 146–152, 155–6, 179–81, 187
  'primitive', 46, 57–8, 68 *et seq.*, 187, 206–7
  literary and spoken, 164–6

Index

Language:
foreign, 46, 172
and thought, 56–8, 60 *et seq.*
Latin Language, 96, 97, 116, 127, 154, 155, 165
Locke, John, 57 n, 62, 64, 72, 73 n, 75, 84, 183 *et seq.*, 206
Logic and Logicians, 60–3, 75, 82, 95, 113 n, 115, 131–2, 131 n, 154, 189 *et seq.*, 205–6
'*Logomorphism*', 90, 146, 184, 187, 193, 196, 204

MACAULAY, 68, 84, 104
Malherbe, 165, 174
Marett, R. R., 83
Maupassant, 115, 116, 131
Meaning, 141, 179–181, 210
defined, 41, 47, 205
dependent on concepts, 48, 49, 55 *et seq.*, 87–8, 188, 189 *et seq.*
opposed to *Definition* (q.v.), 131 n
abstract and concrete, 78 *et seq.*, 94–5, 153, 183 *et seq.*
'inner and outer', 92, 205
physical and psychic, 79 *et seq.*
'given' and created, 102–3, 114–6, 135, 140–1, 143–4
creation of, 50, 65 *et seq.*, 111 *et seq.*, 127 *et seq.*, 140–2, 179
content and reference, 94
English, 117–8, 135–7
Foreign, 133, 172
communicable only by suggestion, 133, 188–9
relation to Myth, 89 *et seq.*, 102–3
in the life of the individual, 82–3, 205–6
of individual words, 60 *et seq* 112 *et seq.*, 127 *et seq.*,
history of study of, 60 *et seq.*, 75
'*Meaning of Meaning*', the, 133–5
Meaningless, the 56–7, 65, 67–8, 86, 131 n, 134
Memory, 56–7, 106, 170
opposed to *Inspiration*, 209–10
Metaphor (see *Resemblances*)
'Radical', 75–82
'Accidental', 122, 197 *et seq.*
assumes self-consciousness, 142–3
'*Metaphorical Period*', the, 73–4, 78, 84, 89
Metaphysicals, the, 51, 98, 173–4
Milton, 45–6, 96–7, 98, 108, 120–1, 124, 128–30, 153–4, 157, 159, 162
Macaulay's Essay on, 84 n
Money, analogy of with words, 61–2
Müller, Max, 57 n, 60, 67, 73–89
Music, 51
of poetry, 47, 99, 150–1, 157,
Mystic, the, 139
Mystics, 210
Myth, 89 *et seq.*, 93 *et seq.*, 102–3, 146–7, 180, 203–4
and *Allegory*, 201

NOIRÉ, Ludwig, 67

OBJECTIVE (see *Subjective*)
Observation defined, 56 n
Order of words, 99, 148–50, 156–8, 162, 185 n

PERCEPT, 193, 193 n, 206–7
defined, 48
and *Idea*, 190–1, 193–5
Perception defined, 56 n
Philology, 60, 63 *et seq.*, 77 *et seq.*, 100–1, 142, 199, 199 n.
Philosophy, 61 *et seq.*, 75, 94–5, 143, 183 *et seq.*, 208 *et seq.*
vocabulary of is metaphorical, 135, 137
Greek, 132–3, 201, 203–4

Pidgin English, 43, 46, 49, 49 n, 70, 171
Plato, 60, 95, 104, 132, 135, 144, 169–70, 180, 196
Pleasure (see *Change*), 159, 162, 171–2, 180–1
 causes of, 47, 152
 a test, 41, 180–1
Poet, the, 50, 102 *et seq*., 131, 135, 159–61, 169–70
 minor, 158–61, 166–7
 attitude of others to, 109–10
Poetic, the, 87 *et seq*., 94 *et seq*., 102 *et seq*., 131–3, 138 *et seq*., 152, 169–70, 178 *et seq*., 189–91, 210–11
 dist. from *Aesthetic*, 170, 178–9
 individualized, 140, 142–3, 144
Poetry :
 'two sorts of', 12, 111–12
 existence of depends on inner experience, 41–2, 49
 and on *Prosaic* principle, 87, 103–4, 105
 defined by Coleridge, 58
 Great, 166, 170, 178 *et seq*. ; defined, 181
 Modern, 33 *et seq*., 148–9, 155–8, 170, 201
 as a possession, 52, 55 *et seq*.
 'joint-stock', 51
 spoken and read, 98–9
 fluid and architectural, 86 *et seq*.
 fashionable contrast with *science*, 63, 138–40
Pope, Alexander, 16, 121, 123, 159, 166 n, 176
Prosaic, the, 87, 94 *et seq*., 111, 114–6, 122–3, 133, 137 n, 138 *et seq*., 145 *et seq*., 152, 168–9, 178 *et seq*., 210–11
 dist, from 'prose', 145 *et seq*.
Psychology, 54, 75, 82 *et seq*., 92, 103, 134–5, 142, 189 *et seq*., 203–6

RALEIGH, Sir Walter, 148, 153, 159
Rational (see *Prosaic*)
Recognition, 56, 189–90
Resemblances (including *Metaphor*, *Simile*, etc,). 55 *et seq*., 63 *et seq*., 87, 103, 111–3, 113 n, 133–4, 140 *et seq*., 186, 197 *et seq*.
Ryhthm, 47, 98 *et seq*., 146 *et seq*., 157–8
Romantic Movement, 124, 135, 164, 180
Roots of speech, 77 *et seq*.
Royal Society, the 166 n.

SANTAYANA, George, 53
'*Science*', 16 *et seq*., 95, 134, 137, 143, 166 n.
 vocabulary of is metaphorical, 135 *et seq*.
 fantasies of pseudo-, 18 *et seq*., 64–5, 74, 78, 90 (and see *France*, Anatole)
 fashionable contrast with *poetry*, 63, 138–40
Seers, 169–70
Self-consciousness, 204–10
 depends on abstract thought, 103, 107, 137 n, 142–3, 179, 204 and *vice versa*, 193 n
 necessary for metaphor-making, 142–3
 produces 'poetry', 103–4 105–6, 178–9
 opposed to inspiration, 109
 opposed to cognition, 208 *et seq*.
 opposed to thinking, 208 *et seq*.
 creation out of full, 110
 unrelieved modern, 126
 Kant and, 192–4, 204
Semantics (see *Bréal*, M., *Meaning* and *Words*)

Shakespeare, 17, 98, 108, 113, 118–20, 126, 128, 130, 135–6, 148
Shelley, 45, 58, 65–6, 67, 68, 86, 87, 105, 108, 135, 148, 155, 167
Simile (see *Resemblances*)
Smith, L. Pearsall, 60
Spengler, Otto, 12–13, 111 n, 133, 138, 207 n
Spenser, Edmund, 117–8, 159, 163–4
'*Spirit*', meaning of connected with that of 'wind' and 'breath', 65–6, 73–4, 79 *et seq.*
Steiner, Rudolf, 12, 184, 195, 207–9
Strangeness, 49, 119–20, 133, 170 *et seq.*, 178–9
Subjective, 203 *et seq.* (and see *Meaning* and *Self-consciousness*)
Synge, J. M., 166 n
Synthesis :
  discursive, 189 *et seq.*, 199
  aesthetic, 189 *et seq.*
Synthetic metaphor, 81
  „ meaning, 123, 190 n

TENNYSON, 124, 156
Trench, Archbishop, 60

'*UN-THINKING*', 133, 134, 206

VEDAS, the 74, 89, 93
Verse, 98, 145 *et seq.*, 152–3
Virgil, 97–8, 127–8

WEST, the, 49, 60–1, 68, 95–6, 111 n, 138, 184, 204
Wisdom, 55, 57, 84, 85, 106–7, 180
Wonder, 177
Words, order of (see *Order*)
  nature of, 50, 61–2, 72–3, 108, 131, 182, 200
  invention of, 112, 130
  'new' uses of, 112–3, 119–20, 124, 130–1
  freshness of, 115
  'souls' of, 115–7, 119, 121
  richness of, 126 (and see *Meaning*)
  unfamiliar, 171 ; 'foreign', 172
  'poetic', 173 ; 'technical', 173 *et seq.*
  semantic histories of, 206
Wordsworth, 58, 106, 121–2, 124, 148 159, 166, 174, 176, 209
  on 'Poetic Diction', 58, 160–3

YOUNG, Edward, 123